CRICKET CONFLICTS
AND CONTROVERSIES
FROM PRE-BODYLINE
TO POST-BOLLYLINE

CRICKET CONFLICTS AND CONTROVERSIES
FROM PRE-BODYLINE TO POST-BOLLYLINE

Kersi Meher-Homji

Foreword by Greg Chappell

Dedicated to the memory of my dear sister Thrity, a lifelong devoted teacher leaving deep imprints on the lives of many, including mine.

CONTENTS

MINI CONFLICTS AND CONTROVERSIES   194

FOREWORD
BY GREG CHAPPELL

Kersi Meher-Homji is a self-confessed cricket tragic. He is a retired research scientist in Virology who was born in India and who has lived in Sydney, Australia, for the past 42 years.

Kersi has written 13 books, including *The Waugh Twins*, *Famous Cricketing Families*, *Out for a Duck*, *Nervous Nineties*, *Six Appeal*, *Heroes of 100 Tests*, *Dramatic Debuts & Swansongs* and *Cricket's Great All-rounders*. This book, his fourteenth, chronicles many of the game's conflicts and controversies from the first Test match to the present day.

I assume that one of the reasons that Kersi asked me to write this foreword is that directly, or indirectly, I have been pretty close to a number of the controversies that he has included in this very readable book.

My grandfather, Vic Richardson, played in the Bodyline series so I was privy to what went on behind the scenes as I grew up. It may have seemed emotional to the public, but it was much more emotional in the dressing room. Players from both sides exchanged words and friendships were strained during that long summer.

I can understand how the players could get so emotional about it for the tactics employed were a huge departure from the norm, but I do have some sympathy for Douglas Jardine.

What Jardine did was to tread the very fine line between playing to the letter of the law and playing within the spirit of the game. He was not the first and, I know, he was not the last.

Yours truly dismayed a few friends on the day that I ordered my brother Trevor to bowl the last delivery of an ODI against New Zealand, underarm. Though it was within the playing conditions, it contravened the spirit of the game. It is the one episode in my career that I regret.

I know that I would do it differently the second time around, but I am not sure if Jardine would have changed a thing. He was prepared to live with his decision, almost as though he had no option, but I do feel for Larwood whose great bowling feats are often overlooked in the drama surrounding Bodyline.

Dennis Lillee and I were in the middle when Ray Illingworth took his team off in Sydney and when Sunil Gavaskar had his tantrum in Melbourne. I was definitely there when Dennis Lillee first displayed his aluminium bat and again when he had his run-in with Javed Miandad. Both events occurred on his home ground in Perth.

Much has been made of my differences with Sourav Ganguly in my time as coach of the Indian team; but not much of it reaches the core of the matter. Once again, emotion has clouded the real story, which was actually quite simple. Sourav was out of form and it was affecting the balance of the team. I tried to reason with Sourav that, if he wanted to save his career, he should consider standing down as captain to focus instead on resurrecting his batting skills. By choosing to ignore that advice, an already difficult situation was exacerbated and the Indian selectors chose to drop him.

Cricket is a wonderful game. It has been blessed with admirable characters and champions throughout its history as well as the odd villain.

In this volume, Kersi Meher-Homji has captured some of the more interesting conflicts and controversies that have interspersed the rich landscape of the game. This book helps to make the game more interesting — and a touch more human in that it shows how emotions can sometimes boil over.

I am certain that you will enjoy it as much as I have.

G.S. Chappell MBE

INTRODUCTION

We say 'It's not cricket' and not 'It's not football or rugby or tennis or swimming or ten-pin bowling'. It is a comment which suggests that cricket embodies all that is noble, decent and law-abiding. As the noted Australian cricket author Ray Robinson wrote in *The Wildest Tests* (1979), 'In the only sport ever called "the noble game", centuries are frequent, coronaries few.'

But in the last few decades, cricket has perhaps witnessed as many conflicts and controversies, on-field clashes and behind the scene drama and trauma as rugby league, football and boxing.

However, controversies in cricket have always been with us, even before the first Test was played in 1877, although not so prominently reported in the daily press. Prior to the Bodyline series of 1932–33 to the 'Bollyline' series of 2007–08 and beyond, through the chucking and ball-tampering accusations of match-fixing, the on-field kicking, bribery and drug-taking allegations, the 'gentle' game of cricket has shown its other side; the dark, murky side.

Despite its past pure village green image, cricket had its turbulent moments even in the 19th century. Cricket was never as spotless and squeaky clean as we would like to believe. Prior to the first ever Test played in March 1877 in Melbourne, England's wicketkeeper Ted Pooley had been 'confiscated' by the authorities in New Zealand on charges of drunken behaviour and heavy gambling. So it was nothing new when 128 years later Australia's Andrew Symonds was sent home from a one-day international (ODI) against Bangladesh in Cardiff, UK, when he turned up drunk on the morning of 18 June 2005.

The purpose of this book is to accurately record cricket's conflicts and controversies, putting them in historic perspective and charting the long term effect these unsavoury events had on the game's evolution.

The Bodyline strategy was planned by England's captain Douglas Jardine in 1932 to combat the invincibility of Don Bradman as a batsman and was executed by one of the deadliest pair of all fast bowlers, Harold Larwood and Bill Voce.

The World Series Cricket (WSC) was the brainchild of Australian television tycoon the late Kerry Packer. He wanted to televise Test cricket on his Channel 9 but the Australian Cricket Board (ACB) would not budge. With the help and expertise of Test greats Richie Benaud, Ian Chappell and Tony Greig, a majority of current Test cricketers were secretly signed in 1977 and the concept of white ball and colour clothing became a reality. This would not have happened if the players were paid properly and the Australian Cricket Board was more flexible.

Not much has changed in two centuries although media scrutiny and tendency to sensationalise incidents has magnified events. In the last few decades you could hardly open a newspaper without the likes of Hansie Cronje, Mohammad Azharuddin, Salim Malik, Muttiah Muralitharan, Shane Warne, Shoaib Akhtar, Harbhajan Singh, Andrew Symonds, Salman Butt, Mohammad Aamer, Mohammad Asif ... not getting involved in conflicts and controversies.

There have been episodes with international flavour like the boycott of South Africa from 1970 to 1991 because of the apartheid policy of its government and the subsequent rebel tours. This boycott was an important contribution to the ending of the policy, which had imposed politics on sport and blighted the lives of millions of black and coloured South Africans.

You cannot talk of cricket without the mention of chucking, which started at the turn of the 20th century, resurfaced in the 1930s, 1950s and 1960s and climaxed with the no-balling of Sri Lankan spinner Muttiah Muralitharan by Australian umpire Darrell Hair in the Melbourne Test of 1995-96.

Hair was embroiled in another controversy during the Oval Test of 2006 between England and Pakistan. After WSC and the above 'forfeited' Test, court appearances for cricketers and cricket organisers have become more common.

Then there were individual player conflicts between Maharajkumar of Vizianagram ('Vizzy') and Lala Amarnath, Dennis Lillee and Javed Miandad, Mike Gatting and Shakoor Rana, Michael Holding and Colin Croft against New Zealand umpires, Steve Waugh and Curtly Ambrose, Greg Chappell and Sourav Ganguly, Harbhajan Singh and Andrew Symonds, Michael Clarke and Simon Katich, the razzle, dazzle and fizzle of IPL, riots in Mumbai, Sydney and Kolkata, and how turbaned Bishan Bedi's decision to 'declare' India's innings in the 1976 Jamaica Test led to reduction on number of bouncers per over. There were also sensations with the 'murder' investigations of a Test cricketer in 2004 in Melbourne, a cricket coach as the 2007 World Cup final ended in darkness; and the tragic fall to death of a prominent cricket author in South Africa in 2011.

So get ready for these controversies in spicy, hot but easy to read chapters.

[1]
SPOT–FIXING AT LORD'S PUT THREE CRICKETERS IN JAIL

To me, one of the highlights of a Sydney Test in the last few years has been the dinner hosted by The Australian Cricket Media Association (ACMA) usually on day–3 of the Test to present the Australian Cricketer of the Year Award at the Sydney Football Stadium.

Australia was on her knees that day. It was not a question as to will they lose the Test against Pakistan on 5 January 2010, but when will they lose it. The Australian journalists appeared dejected, which is to be expected, but surprisingly, so were their Pakistani counterparts.

I sat on the same table with the visiting journalists, introduced myself and said, 'Let me be the first to congratulate you guys.'

'Why?' was their gloomy response.

'Because Pakistan will win sometime tomorrow afternoon with a day to spare and level the series one–all', I added.

'Don't be too sure', one of them mumbled. 'Australians are fighters and Pakistan is Pakistan. They self–destruct.'

'They snatch defeat from the jaws of victory', commented another. In view of what happened the following day, their predictions proved spot on.

> *'Because Pakistan will win sometime tomorrow afternoon with a day to spare and level the series one–all', I added. 'Don't be too sure', one of them mumbled. 'Australians are fighters and Pakistan is Pakistan. They self–destruct.'*

So let us revisit the topsy–turvy Sydney Test of January 2010. It was a gloomy and wet morning when Ricky Ponting won the toss and surprisingly decided to bat on a green wicket. He must have regretted it as Australia was bowled out for 127 in 44.2 overs, Ponting scoring a duck and fast–medium bowler Mohammad Asif grabbing 6 for 41.

Pakistani openers Imran Farhat and Salman Butt almost overtook the Australian total by adding 109 on a pitch that was improving by the hour. They were at one stage 2 for 205, a lead of 78 runs with eight wickets in hand. Eventually they totalled 333 to be 206 runs in front.

At stumps on the third day, Australia was 8 for 286 despite opener Shane Watson's 97. They were just 80 runs ahead with only tail–enders to support a resolute Mike Hussey, unbeaten on 73.

The expected early breakthroughs did not come the next morning as Hussey and the number 10 batsman Peter Siddle added 123 runs for the ninth wicket, 94 of them on the fourth day before Siddle was dismissed. The pair was lucky because Pakistan wicketkeeper Kamran Akmal dropped four fairly easy catches, three of them enabling Man of the Match Hussey to make an unbeaten 134. The other dropped catch helped Siddle to make 38, then his highest Test score. The bowler to suffer from these lapses was leg-spinner Danish Kaneria who despite poor catching finished with 5 for 151 as Australia totalled 381.

What surprised the critics and commentators was that instead of going for the kill on the morning of the fourth day of the Test, Pakistan captain, the bearded Mohammad Yousuf, set an overly defensive field.

Set only 176 runs to win, a lacklustre Pakistan was dismissed for 139 to lose by 36 runs, an astonishing turn around. Only five times in the history of Test cricket had a team won after a first innings deficit of more than 200 runs. The words of the Pakistani journalists uttered nineteen hours earlier at the Media Night were ringing in my ears, especially the phrases 'self-destruct' and 'snatching defeat from the jaws of victory'.

Eyebrows were raised and the general attitude was that of nudge-nudge, wink-wink. But according to Cricket Australia there was nothing suspicious. Was it one of cricket's glorious uncertainties or inglorious certainties?

Here are the views of David Jenkins, the author of *Near Death on the Sub-continent – The Gavin Stevens Story* and other titles, on this contentious Sydney Test in a personal letter:

At lunch time on the fourth and last day, with Hussey and Siddle still in and a century partnership to boot, I asked Channel 9 commentator and former Australian captain Mark Taylor if he could have imagined this lunch-time score at the start of play that day. His response was, 'Not before play–but as soon as I saw those field placings, I could imagine this result.'

During this break it was also freely mentioned in the media room that Shane Warne was so confident Pakistan would win and win quickly he had booked an early flight to Melbourne. Now, with Australia still batting he had to cancel his plans and stay in Sydney. With Hussey being dropped on a seemingly regular basis, and a missed run-out on top of those dropped catches, it looked like Pakistan had been very generous to say the least.

I watched the last hour or so with an English newspaper journalist (name and paper not remembered) who watched in astonishment as Pakistan crumbled to an amazing loss by 36 runs. An hour from the finish we were talking about the Pakistan wicket procession when he said, 'Don't you get the smell of corruption about this game?' I agreed that it did not look good and he then said, 'These players should be banned for life—this is outrageous. Those field settings this morning for Siddle showed they did not want to get him out.'

Again, I nodded my agreement and he added, 'If they had dismissed Siddle, or Hussey—who was missed several times—even Pakistan could not have explained a loss chasing sixty or seventy. By allowing Australia a lead of nearly two hundred they can now deliberately lose honourably!'

While the thoughts had been going round my head for some time, and certainly since that comment by Mark Taylor, I was still trying to think of it as just a miracle win. My English friend helped me think more clearly about what was happening in front of me—and it wasn't a good feeling.

Subsequently, Kamran was accused of deliberately underperforming during Pakistan's surprise defeat against Australia in the above Test, where he failed to run out Shane Watson besides those four dropped catches. Despite the allegations, Kamran claimed to have a clearance letter from the ICC saying he is not being investigated.

He also vowed to clear his name through the integrity committee, which reportedly asked for details of his assets and bank accounts. He was axed from the team after a dismal performance behind the stumps at the 2011 World Cup where he dropped New Zealand's Ross Taylor twice in one over from fast bowler Shoaib Akhtar.

Seven months after the 2010 Sydney Test, the fourth and final Test at Lord's between England and Pakistan in August became notorious for spot-fixing by the Pakistanis. It plunged cricket into its most unusual corruption crisis. This, however, had passed almost unnoticed during the first two days of this headline-making Test.

In the first 20 overs of England's first innings (split over two days because of rain) Pakistan's teenage fast bowler Mohammad Aamer bowled two no-balls and his new-ball partner Mohammad Asif bowled one no-ball. With Aamer capturing

6 for 84 and England at one stage 7 for 102, the significance of these no–balls was not noticed.

But the magnitude of those no–balls came out in the open on the evening of the third day, 28 August, when the *News of the World (NOTW)* tabloid alleged that Pakistan captain Salman Butt and quickies Aamer and Asif had colluded with Butt's agent Mazhar Majeed to deliver three no–balls in a predetermined order in exchange for £150 000.

The allegation was not for match–fixing but for its evil stepsister, spot–fixing. In spot–fixing, items like extras (including no–balls) take place at the appointed time for the benefit of gamblers and bookmakers, mostly from Asia. It focuses on event–specific markets known as 'brackets'.

The allegations were backed by audio and video footage, including damning evidence, in which Majeed counted out £140 000 in cash while discussing the spot–fixing. The footage was filmed during a series of meetings before the Lord's Test. Acting on a tip–off from a former member of the Pakistan team management, *NOTW*'s investigations editor posed as a representative for an Asian betting syndicate.

According to *NOTW*, Mazhar Majeed claimed to represent Indian bookmakers specialising in offering odds on 10–over brackets. He also stated that he represented at least six of the Pakistani touring squad including skipper Butt. Majeed also admitted his involvement in numerous 'fixed matches' including the January 2010 Sydney Test. However, the Sydney Test was declared clean according to the findings of Cricket Australia and the ICC.

It was shocking as the above three Test cricketers were arrested for spot–fixing. Captain Butt was defiant as he said on 29 August 2010, the final day of the Test, 'These are just allegations. Anyone can stand up and say things about you; it does not make them true.'

Coming back to the August 2010 Lord's Test: The first two alleged transgression—no–balls by Aamer–occurred on the rain–interrupted first day when play was limited to only 12.3 overs in the afternoon. According to Scyld Berry in *Wisden 2011,* 'At 1.56 p.m. Aamer delivered a no–ball as the first ball of the second over from the Pavilion End–the third over of England's innings–as predicted. The left-armer was a foot beyond the line of the popping crease, a remarkable distance.'

Aamer spent time examining the spikes of his right shoe and Butt brought in some sawdust in his cupped hands to create the impression that the ground was slippery, which did not seem so in reality. From the Nursery End, Asif delivered a no-ball for what would have been the last over of his five-over spell. Shortly afterwards the play was abandoned for the day. Unknowingly, the spectators had witnessed a different type of cricket corruption; spot-fixing.

Aamer bowled magnificently on the second morning, dismissing batsmen numbers 4, 5 and 6 (Kevin Pietersen, Paul Collingwood and Eoin Morgan) for ducks and at one stage his figures were four wickets for no run off only 8 balls. However, before this spell, Butt had walked up to Aamer at the start of his run-up and whispered something in his ear. Aamer's third ball of his third over was a no-ball, again a foot past the popping crease, which shocked the TV cricket commentator and former great West Indies fast bowler Michael Holding who exclaimed 'Wow!' in disbelief.

No-balls are part and parcel of cricket but the foot landing that far off the target bordered on unbelievable and appeared contrived, especially as the bowler is normally so accurate. At stumps on the third day the Pakistanis heard of the *News of the World* story. Soon the police arrived at Lord's to conduct inquiries.

The next day, cricket was furthest away from the Pakistanis' minds and they were dismissed for 74 and 147. Pakistan lost the Test by a huge margin of an innings and 225 runs and the series 1-3.

The presentation ceremony was conducted not on the field but discreetly in the Pavilion. Giles Clarke, the chairman of England and Wales Cricket Board, refused to shake Aamer's hand after he was adjudged Pakistan's Man of the Series. The police then took over conducting inquiries at Pakistan's team hotel and confiscating the mobile phones of Butt, Asif and Aamer.

According to *NOTW*, the no-ball spot-fixing was 'the most sensational sporting scandal ever', producing video tapes showing large amounts of money changing hands.

It was shocking as the above three Test cricketers were arrested for spot-fixing. Captain Butt was defiant as he said on 29 August 2010, the final day of the Test, 'These are just allegations. Anyone can stand up and say things about you;

it does not make them true.'

But the video evidence presented by *NOTW* was convincing. The tainted trio did not play the remaining matches on the tour. In December that year Butt claimed that the £29 000 found in his London hotel room consisted of his tour and entertainment allowances and advance payment for bat sponsorship as well as moneys for opening an ice-cream parlour.

Below were the findings of the ICC's Independent Anti-Corruption Tribunal in February 2011:

- Mohammad Aamer agreed to bowl, and did bowl, two deliberate no-balls in the Lord's Test.
- Mohammad Asif agreed to bowl, and did bowl, a deliberate no-ball in the same Test.
- Salman Butt was party to the bowling of those deliberate no-balls.

Now to the aftermath of the 2010 'no-ball' Lord's Test saga two years later in 2012.

According to his lawyer Yasin Patel, Butt—convicted for 30 months—travelled back to Pakistan after being released from prison after seven months. His release under the government's early release scheme for foreign nationals meant he had been formally deported from the UK and that he couldn't return to England for 10 years.

Cricinfo quoted Patel saying that Butt would begin rebuilding his life and hoped to return to cricket:

His return back home will allow Butt to spend time with his family and relatives. He will get to see and hold his son who he has not seen since his birth in November 2011. He can now return to his homeland, start to rebuild his reputation and begin the long process in his efforts to return back to top-level cricket.

When asked specifically by the noted Indian correspondent Bipin Dani whether Butt was deported from England, Patel replied firmly, 'Salman Butt is not deported but is willingly returning to his country.'

Meanwhile, Asif was released after serving six months of his 12-month prison term but he remained in the UK planning his appeal against a seven-year ban from cricket. Aamer served three months in a young offenders' institute.

The jury in the spot-fixing trial at Southwark Crown Court had found Butt and Asif guilty by a unanimous verdict on the charge of 'conspiracy to cheat' and guilty by a 10–2 majority decision on the charge of 'conspiracy to obtain and accept corrupt payments'. Aamer pleaded guilty. Butt was the last of the three Pakistan players to be released.

Named as the 'orchestrator' of the spot–fixing, Butt was described as a 'malign influence' on his teammates Aamer and Asif.

Asif was released from Canterbury Prison in south–east England in May 2012 after completing half of his one year sentence for spot–fixing. He was still under a seven–year ban (the last two years of which are suspended) imposed by the ICC tribunal. His international career seems finished. According to Dani, Asif was spared from electronic tagging, a practice adopted by prisons in UK allowing their whereabouts to be monitored.

Aamer was released in February 2012 after serving half of a six–month sentence. He admitted his guilt and promised to put the past behind him. Also, he later worked with the ICC in the production of an anti–corruption video. He was banned for five years and, at 20 years of age, has worked with a psychologist Maqbool 'Max' Babri to look towards the future rather than the murky past.

Mazhar Majeed, the agent who was accused of setting up the deal uncovered by the *NOTW* sting operation, was imprisoned for 32 months in 2011. As we go to press he is the only one of the conspirators still in prison.

ONE MORE SKELETON WAS LOCATED IN the locker. In June 2012, Pakistan leg–spinner Danesh Kaneria was banned for life and branded a liar and a 'grave danger' to the game as the English and Wales Cricket Board (ECB) handed down severe punishments at the end of county cricket's first corruption case. The case arose from events at a 40–over match for Essex in 2009.

Mervyn Westfield, Kaneria's former Essex teammate and accomplice in the scam, was suspended for five years but escaped a life ban by pleading guilty to a fixing charge and agreeing to join anti–corruption education programmes. Kaneria received a life ban for his role as a corrupter.

Kaneira proclaimed his innocence. But 'backed by phone and text message records, the [ECB] panel was satisfied that Kaneria introduced Westfield to two Asian businessmen involved in illegal gambling', reported *The Telegraph*, London.

2

TED POOLEY IMPRISONED
BEFORE THE INAUGURAL 1877 TEST

W|e tend to think that gambling, illegal betting, bribery, match-fixing, spot-fixing and other corruptions are modern phenomena. Far from it! They have been with us for the past two centuries, and are as old as cricket itself. Among the first person to be kicked out of cricket for match-fixing was William Lambert in June 1817. That is almost 200 years ago, and 180 years before Salim Malik, Hansie Cronje, Mohammad Azharuddin, Salman Butt, Mohammad Asif and Mohammad Aamer put cricketing vices on the front pages of newspapers in the 1990s and early 2000s.

True, the more things change, the more they remain the same.

Dave Liverman, a Professor of History in Yale University, wrote in *Cricinfo* 'A great cricketer in the early days of the organised game, Lambert was a fine exponent of the forward style of batting and was regarded as one of the best batsman in England.' Lambert was the first batsman in cricket history to score centuries in both innings of a match, for Sussex at Epsom in 1817, a feat not repeated for 76 years. A few months later he was banned from playing any matches at Lord's for not trying his best in a match for England against Nottinghamshire. Perhaps it was an early form of match-fixing. An efficient bowler and an agile fielder he made his living from cricket, playing for the highest bidder, mostly in single and double wicket matches.

In the 1820s, the cricket authorities drove the bookies out of Lord's and matches thrown for large amount of money became only an unpleasant memory. However, betting on a small scale continued but posed no threat to the integrity of the game, according to David Underdown in **Cricinfo.**

In the 1820s, the cricket authorities drove the bookies out of Lord's and matches thrown for large amount of money became only an unpleasant memory. However, betting on a small scale continued but posed no threat to the integrity of the game, according to David Underdown in *Cricinfo*.

Test cricket's first gambling victim was Ted Pooley, an excellent wicketkeeper and a compulsive gambler. A long-serving Surrey professional, handsome Pooley was selected to tour New Zealand and Australia with James Lillywhite's team in 1876–77 as a first choice wicketkeeper. His love for making money at every opportunity; however, was his undoing. 'It was chasing a quick buck that led to his being marooned in Christchurch, New Zealand, as England and Australia met for the first time at Melbourne,' Martin Williamson wrote in *Cricinfo* in 2011.

Not that this was his first offence. Surrey had suspended Pooley in 1873 after an incident at Bramall Lane in Sheffield where stories were floating that he had taken a bet and there were reports that money had changed hands. The suspension did not teach him a lesson as he continued with his gambling in New Zealand three years later. There, most of the matches were games against odds, for example playing XXII of Auckland and XVIII of Canterbury. Betting appeared official as odds were published in local papers.

In those days it was acceptable to predict the scores for each player in a side, with very good odds on offer. Ralph Donkin, a railway engineer who was staying in town, made such an offer, with odds to anyone exactly predicting each batsman's individual total.

While in Canterbury he met local 'bookies' and thought of a scheme to make easy money. In those days it was acceptable to predict the scores for each player in a side, with very good odds on offer. Ralph Donkin, a railway engineer who was staying in town, made such an offer, with odds to anyone exactly predicting each batsman's individual total. In 'odds' matches, low scores were normal. Half a dozen opposing teams had already been bowled out for under 50 on the tour and Pooley, therefore, wagered a certain amount per batsman that each of their individual scores would be zero.

Canterbury's innings produced 11 ducks and so he was entitled to collect £36. But Donkin refused to pay up, stating that he had witnesses to substantiate his claim that he had declared the bet off before the game.

That evening Pooley confronted Donkin in the smoking room of their hotel and argued heatedly. A little while later, as Donkin and a friend headed out to a theatre, it was alleged that Pooley ambushed him and hit him three times in the face. When Donkin returned to his hotel he found, according to the *North Otago Star*, 'every particle of his wearing apparel torn to shreds'.

Pooley moved on with Lillywhite's team to Dunedin but trouble followed him. While on the pitch he was constantly distracted by telegrams demanding his return to Christchurch. He initially refused but at the end of the match Pooley and Alfred Bramhall, the baggage man, were arrested in connection with the assault and released on bail but told not to travel. The remainder of Lillywhite's party went on ahead.

A Christchurch magistrate judged that Pooley had thrown the first blow in the altercation with Donkin and fined him £5 for assault. Pooley was not in serious trouble but out of pocket. However, Donkin laid another charge, accusing him of wilfully and maliciously destroying his property, including important plans relating to his work. The magistrate committed the pair to trial, and although the hearing was scheduled for a week later, the case was adjourned when the defence requested a witness be brought from Melbourne.

> *The local press expected a custodial sentence. 'It is felt Pooley ... will get three months and is deserving of punishment for his dastardly conduct [but] no sympathy is expressed for Donkin who it is generally felt should have paid a bet that he made with his eyes open.'*

The local press expected a custodial sentence. 'It is felt Pooley ... will get three months and is deserving of punishment for his dastardly conduct [but] no sympathy is expressed for Donkin who it is generally felt should have paid a bet that he made with his eyes wide open.'

By the time the case was heard in Christchurch's Supreme Court on 6 April 1877, Pooley and Bramhall had been on bail for four weeks, the Melbourne witness had not appeared, and the historic match (later termed as the inaugural Test) in Melbourne had been over for a fortnight.

While the evidence against the pair was largely circumstantial, a waiter told the court that Pooley had instructed him to tell Donkin that 'if he sleeps there [in his room] tonight he'll find himself half-dead in the morning.' But other witnesses said they had heard other members of the England side tell Donkin 'we will have it out of you by the morning.'

Donkin hardly helped his case by claiming that he believed a bet could be cancelled if it subsequently emerged the odds were against one of the parties. The jury was unconvinced, and took less than an hour to return a not-guilty verdict.

Remarkably, the treatment of Pooley and Bramhall had resulted in residents of Christchurch taking pity on them, and they organised a whip–round that raised £50 for the Englishmen and a gold ring for Pooley.

Pooley eventually landed back in England on 9 July 1877, almost a month after the rest of his teammates and two months after the birth of his second child.

Australia won the inaugural Test in Melbourne in March 1877 by 45 runs, English–born Australian opener Charles Bannerman scored 165 retired hurt. A shattered Pooley returned home alone. He was then 35 and never played a Test. In his exile he earned good money playing minor cricket but died bankrupt in a London workhouse in 1907 aged 65.

According to *The Wisden Book of Cricketers' Lives* (1986), 'He was in many ways his own enemy, but even to the last he had a geniality and sense of humour that to a certain extent condoned his weaknesses.'

Fancy, the hassles he went through for a bet of £36, a trifling amount now but a large sum of money then. Some of the modern scandals of bribery and match–fixing would pale in comparison to the Pooley tear–jerker. Just as a feature film on Hansie Cronje was shot in 2008, a full–length movie on Pooley titled *What Odds*, I'll bet again with violence in bars would not be a bad idea.

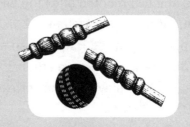

3

THE ABORIGINAL
CONNECTIONS AND
DISCONNECTIONS

A ustralian Aborigines have been playing cricket since the 1830s but only in small numbers. Why this has been so and why only one has gone on to play Test cricket remains a cultural mystery. He is Jason Gillespie, the one with the bouncing mullet and Dennis Lillee–like glare when bowling. Selected as a fast bowler he scored 1218 runs at 18.73 and took 259 wickets at 26.13 in 71 Tests from 1996 to 2006. His only Test century was an unbeaten double hundred (201) against Bangladesh at Chittagong in April 2006. This was in his final Test innings and remains as the highest score by a night watchman. He was adjudged Man of the Match and Man of the Series but the 31 year old was never picked again in a Test or a one–day international (ODI) since then. It was a unique swan song.

The great-grandson of a Kamilaroi warrior, Gillespie occupies a significant niche in Australian history as the only acknowledged Aboriginal Test cricketer. Were there other Aborigines worthy of wearing the baggy green?

Daniel Christian with an Aboriginal heritage, being from the Wiradjuri tribe in New South Wales, is a graduate of Cricket Australia's indigenous cricket program, captaining the national indigenous development squad during a tour of England in 2009. In 14 ODIs for Australia, the 29 year old has scored 227 runs at 22.70 and has taken 15 wickets at 26.40 as at July 2012.

The great-grandson of a Kamilaroi warrior, Gillespie occupies a significant niche in Australian history as the only acknowledged Aboriginal Test cricketer. Were there other Aboriginals worthy of wearing the baggy green?

The Aborigines, however, have produced competent cricketers in the distant past, namely Johnny Mullagh, Albert Henry, Jack Marsh, Eddie Gilbert (who once dismissed Don Bradman for a duck in 1931). Also some tragic stories are related about them, like the one on the first Aboriginal cricketer Shiney or Shinal. He played in 1835 but on his death was beheaded and the 'specimen' was sent to an Irish museum for preservation. *The Oxford Companion to Australian Cricket* (1996) edited by Richard Cashman, Warwick Franks, Jim Maxwell, Brian Stoddart, Amanda Weaver and Ray Webster gives detailed information on the role of Aborigines in Australian cricket.

Coached by Tom Wills, an Aboriginal team toured England in 1868 with Charles Lawrence as its manager, 10 years before the first white Australian team. According to Greg de Moore in *Tom Wills – His spectacular Rise and Tragic Fall* (2008), Wills was a flawed genius, fearless leader and the man often credited with creating the game we now know as the Australian Rules football. Wills was a noble soul. He experienced first–hand the devastating effect of racial tension when his father and 18 other Europeans were killed by local Aboriginal people on the family property in Central Queensland. Yet five years later, Wills coached the 1886 Aboriginal team to England.

In *Cricket Walkabout* (1988), John Mulvaney and Rex Harcourt have written authoritatively on the 1868 pioneering Aboriginal cricket tour to England. The team played 47 matches from May to October, winning 14, losing 14 with 19 drawn. The Board for the Protection of Aborigines were worried about their safety and feared that the team might be abandoned in England. There was a tragedy; King Cole died during the tour while Sundown and Jim Crow became so ill that they were sent home.

However, four of the players made outstanding contributions on that tour. A large burly man, Harry Bullocky, performed so well that the English critics thought he was good enough to play county cricket. Twopenny took 35 wickets on the tour at an excellent average of 6.90 but was labelled a chucker. A tiny man, Johnny Cuzens made 1367 runs at 18.48 and took 114 wickets at 11.37.

Dubbed the 'black WG of the team', Johnny Mullagh (original name Unamurriman) played 43 matches in England, scoring 1677 runs at 23.85 and capturing 245 wickets at 10.16. He later played for Victoria against Lord Harris's English team. After the tour, Mullagh and Cuzens were employed as professionals by the Melbourne Cricket Club.

Another talented Aboriginal cricketer was Albert (Alec) Henry. From Deebing Creek, near Ipswich, he was an all–rounder, shining out in rugby union as well as sprinting, and was the first Aborigine to play first–class cricket for Queensland. The English tourists in 1903–04 described him as a frighteningly fast bowler. He was no–balled for throwing in Brisbane grade cricket but spoke for himself at what he saw as unfair treatment by the umpire. Later, his outspokenness against white authority saw him charged with 'loafing, malingering and defying authority', following which he was forcibly removed to far north Queensland. He died of tuberculosis at the age of 29, a defiant victim of the system.

Jack Marsh, a controversial fast bowler from New South Wales, had problems with State umpires, despite proving his action was legitimate. Publication *The Referee* wrote, 'he had gifts no other man in Australia—probably no other bowler in the world—possesses: he curves the ball, he bowls a peculiar dropping ball, and his breakback on a perfect wicket is phenomenal for a bowler of his pace.'

An Englishman on the 1903–04 tour commented that he was the fastest bowler in the world, with a legal action. Colin Tatz, the author of *Obstacle Race: Aborigines in Sport* (1995) wrote:

Monty Noble, a Test selector [as indeed a Test great] felt that Marsh 'did not have class enough to play representative matches ...' Writer and cricketer L.O.S. Poidevin commented that Marsh would not be picked for Australia 'because of the absurd white Australia policy had tainted the hearts of the rules of cricket' and legendary batsman Warren Bardsley declared 'the reason they kept him out of big cricket was his colour.'

Marsh played six first-class matches for New South Wales, taking 34 wickets at 21.47 from 1900–03. He was battered to death in a street in Orange, New South Wales, in 1916. His killers were charged with manslaughter and not murder, the judge Bevan opined that Marsh might have deserved it.

In 1931, Queenslander Eddie Gilbert, a dynamic fast bowler, dismissed Don Bradman for a duck from a run-up of only four to five paces. Bradman later wrote, 'he sent down in that period the fastest bowling I can remember ... One delivery knocked the bat out of my hand and I unhesitatingly class this short burst faster than anything seen from [Harold] Larwood or anyone else'. In that match Gilbert took 4 for 74 off 21 overs. In 23 first-class matches he captured 87 wickets at 28.97. Yet no Test call for him, despite the fact that only Test bowler Tim Wall, had a better record as an opening bowler during Gilbert's career. Also, as the rest of his teammates travelled to match venues and back by cars he had to travel by train.

Unfortunately, newspapers those days did not invoke the word racism as they do now and report it at the drop of a hat even when not justified. Controversies are highly exaggerated these days.

[4]
TEAM BOYCOTT
OF THE 1885
MELBOURNE
TEST

Let me assure those who describe cricketers who joined World Series Cricket in 1977 as 'mercenaries' that this was not the first time cricketers had protested against poor payment. Boxers, footballers and tennis players have always been paid so fabulously well, so why aren't Test cricketers (who are in action for a far longer period of time)? Test cricket was in its infancy when all 11 Australian cricketers boycotted the 1885 Melbourne Ashes Test. That was 92 years before Kerry Packer improved the financial situation of cricketers worldwide.

Australia's team showed 11 changes as all the cricketers who had played the first Test in Adelaide a fortnight previously demanded 50 per cent of the gate money for the second Test in Melbourne starting on New Year's Day 1885. Not surprisingly, the newlook XI lost by an innings to England. With the striking cricketers back in the fold, Australia won the next Test in Sydney.

Here is the background to the player boycott in the 1885 Melbourne Test. Ill-feeling between Australian and English cricketers over the issue of gate money led to a season of turmoil in 1884–85. It had started during Australia's tour of England in 1884 where they lost the three Test series 0–1. The highlight for the touring team was their skipper Billy Murdoch scoring Test cricket's first double century, 211, at The Oval in August 1884. However, the London newspaper the *World* was critical of the attitude of the tourists. 'The Australians make their own terms, insist on them, not always gracefully, and they play obviously for the money's sake.' The newspaper suggested that they should call themselves 'professionals'.

Australia's team showed eleven changes as all the cricketers who had played the first Test in Adelaide a fortnight prior demanded 50 per cent of the gate money for the second Test in Melbourne starting on New Year 1885. Not surprisingly, the newlook XI lost by an innings to England. With the striking cricketers back in the fold, Australia won the next Test in Sydney.

Jack Pollard wrote in *The Complete Illustrated History of Australian Cricket* (1992), 'The 1884 Australians refused to be labelled and none of the players who followed them in national touring teams wanted to be regarded as "amateurs" or "professionals" but simply as "cricketers".' When the Australians heard of the fees their manager / publicist / agent John Conway had negotiated for the Englishmen, they refused to play unless they received more pay. They demanded excess gate receipts to go into their pockets rather than to colony associations after the Englishmen had been paid.

They were embittered at the action of English professionals Arthur Shrewsbury, William Barnes and Wilfred Flowers, who had refused to play for the Players against the tourists at Sheffield in 1884. These players were included in the English touring squad to Australia a few months later, with Shrewsbury as the captain and co-organiser of the tour. The Australians, except Fred Spofforth who was injured, took their revenge by refusing to play for their State teams against the tourists prior to the Test matches.

The Australians also demanded 50 per cent of the gate money from the first Test in Adelaide. It was a historic occasion as it was the first ever Test played in Adelaide. But it was a financial disaster and the South Australian Cricket Association lost heavily after giving a guarantee of a flat 450 pounds to both teams. For the following Test in Melbourne the Victorian Cricket Association took a tougher stance and refused the Australians' their money demands, and hence their en-masse withdrawal from the Melbourne Test.

The new look Australian team (with nine Test debutants) lost by 10 wickets. Only two, Sammy Jones and Tom Horan, had Test experience. Appointed as a crisis captain, Horan made a bitter attack on Murdoch's 'striking' eleven:

> The public desires to see the best team in Australia meet the Englishmen, but rather than please the public these men prefer to vent their spite by doing all in their power to keep the pounds out of the pockets of our English professional visitors who make their living by playing cricket ... They have shown no manliness, no courtesy, no spark of kindly feeling whatever to our English friends.

By the same token, one may argue, weren't the majority of the Australian cricketers also professionals, although they called themselves 'cricketers'?

The discord brought decline as disputes over match fees, intercolonial rivalry and an occasional physical conflict among representative players brought failures on the field. And we now say how united and unselfish cricketers were in the past!

English cricket historian Harry Altham concluded, 'The great strength of Australian cricket was sapped for year after year by internal argument.' Another English cricket writer 'Felix' (real name Nicholas Wanostrocht) was more outspoken, when he wrote in *The Australian* that cricket had come under 'a deep and lasting shadow, which cast a universal gloom upon our manly game.' It was a reflection of the general feeling of Australian cricket followers.

The Sydney riot of 1879

NEW SOUTH WALES COLONY XI CAPTAINED by W.M. 'Billy' Murdoch, played an England XI captained by Lord Harris at the Association ground in Sydney's Moore Park. Each team chose an umpire, England went for 22-year-old Victorian George Coulthard; New South Wales chose Edmund Barton.

With England needing only a few wickets for victory, Murdoch was given run out by Coulthard. This prompted 2000 outraged larrikins to storm the ground, convinced that the Victorian umpire Coulthard was in cahoots with the English.

Lord Harris was hit with a stick, rioters cracked whips. England fielder A.N. Hornby had his shirt ripped off his back and fieldsmen armed themselves with stumps. One spectator, A.B. 'Banjo' Patterson, told tales of the riot when Barton became Australia's first Prime Minister.

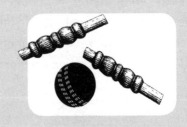

[5]
COMING TO
BLOWS IN
1911–12 STYLE

C lem Hill's name is associated with that of the legendary Vic Trumper. Immortals at the turn of the 20th century, their mighty deeds are recalled after over a hundred years.

When he was 16, Hill played a remarkable innings of 360 in an Inter-College match in Adelaide in 1893. This was the highest individual score in Australia at that time and young Hill gave clear indication of things to come in future. Australia's first great left-hander, he became the first batsman to score 99 in Test cricket (against England in Melbourne in 1901–02) and followed it up in the next Test in Adelaide with 98 and 97. In 49 Tests he scored 3412 runs at 39.21 with seven centuries and six nineties. Powerfully built, his footwork was nimble and he had all the strokes in the book. A legend in his lifetime, he went on to become one of the immortals in the game.

But in 1912, he showed his belligerent side as he was involved in an ugly controversy, a fist fight no less. During the 1911–12 Test series, he was at the centre of growing tensions between a number of senior players and the Australian Board of Control over the issue of who was going to control Australian cricket. These tensions were enhanced by the strong personal antipathy between Hill and Peter McAlister, a stylish opening batsman with a poor Test record. It exploded on the issue of selection of the Australian squad to England in 1912.

Australia's on-field performance in the 1911–12 series was pathetic. After winning the first Test in Sydney they lost the next four to surrender the Ashes. The Australian morale was also eroded by the off-field clashes with the administrators.

The conflict continued throughout the season and culminated in a 20-minute fist fight between Hill and McAlister during the selection of the team for the fourth Test. The root of this conflict was the ongoing struggle between the cricketers and administrators for the control of the

But in 1912, he showed his belligerent side as he was involved in an ugly controversy, a fist fight no less. During the 1911–12 Test series, he was at the centre of growing tensions between a number of senior players and the Australian Board of Control over the issue of who was going to control Australian cricket.

The Board and the players had been at odds for a decade. Three years later the two were national selectors. Hill was also the Test captain. McAlister had made a series of disrespectful comments about Hill, privately and in the media, suggesting that Hill should drop himself from the side.

organisation and financial management of tours to and from Australia.

Earlier in 1909, according to Brydon Coverdale in *Cricinfo*, McAlister had upset his teammates by effectively acting as a spy for the Cricket Board during the tour to England. The Board and the players had been at odds for a decade. Three years later the two were national selectors. Hill was also the Test captain. McAlister had made a series of disrespectful comments about Hill, privately and in the media, suggesting that Hill should drop himself from the side. The animosity came to a head at a selection meeting in the Board of Control's Sydney office. Depending on which report is to be believed, Hill either slapped or punched McAlister, and a 20-minute brawl ensued, with Hill almost throwing his opponent out of a third-storey window. After it was all over, Hill went back to his hotel and the meeting continued.

Australian Test cricketer and later a selector, Frank Iredale, was one of the witnesses of the fight and said that both combatants were game and determined. A blow-by-blow account of the brawl was published in *The Australian* in 1911. It stated that they fought fiercely. Locked in each others' arms, they swayed round the room, crashing against table and walls. 'They went at it hammer and tongs,' concluded Iredale who was pinned in a corner by the table.

As a consequence to this fracas, six topnotch Australian players—Hill, Trumper, Warwick Armstrong, Vernon Ransford, Hanson 'Sammy' Carter and Albert 'Tibby' Cotter—declined to tour England in 1912 for the Triangular Test tournament between England, Australia and South Africa. Hill never played in a Test again.

His end was tragic. He died at the age of 68 from injuries sustained when he was thrown from a tram in a Melbourne traffic accident in 1945.

'Crock, Crock, Crock' chanted the angry Sydney crowd

CLEM HILL WAS THE CAUSE OF one of the angriest crowd demonstrations known to Australian cricket. When playing against England in the 1903 Sydney Test, he and Trumper ran four from a drive from Trumper off Leon Braund with Hill running past the stumps at the bowler's end. When overthrows resulted, Hill had to turn back and run the length of the pitch. The mid-on fielder Albert Relf threw to the wicketkeeper 'Dick' Lilley and umpire Bob Crockett declared Hill out as he passed the stumps. Hill strongly objected to this decision as he was sure he was in. Spectators threw bottles on the cycle track that encircled the ground. Amid the uproar that followed, Crockett had to be escorted from the field by police. English captain 'Plum' Warner threatened to take his team off as cries of 'Crock, Crock, Crock' echoed around the SCG.

Oh for a DRS (Decision Review System) then!

THE BODYLINE
FURORE

Controversies in cricket have become a regular event these days, rarely a month passing without a cricketing headline of the wrong type. But they are minor compared to the Bodyline furore of 1932–33, the Olympics of mega controversies.

It happened much before I was born but I grew up seeing Harold Larwood's photograph on the wall of my parent's home in Udwada, India. Larwood, the English fast bowler who made the legendary Australian batsman Don Bradman look mortal for one series, was my eldest brother Behram's idol.

Also, my uncle, Kharshed Meher-Homji who had played one Test against England in 1936 at Manchester, had hit Larwood for four fours in 5 balls in a match for Parsees against Europeans at Bombay Gymkhana in India in 1936. He never stopped talking about it till he passed away in 1982 aged 70. So I had virtually grown up knowing the name of Larwood.

'Lol' Larwood had a big chuckle when I related these incidents to him while visiting and chatting with him at his home in the Sydney suburb of Randwick in 1980. He was 76 then, yet his handshake was so firm that I almost shouted 'Ouch'. We chatted about Bradman, 'Obbs' (Hobbs), 'Sootcliff' [Sutcliff], Lindwall, fast bowlers of his time and in 1970s, World Series Cricket, his life in Australia, his family.

So well known is the Bodyline series that my wife who knew nothing of cricket till she met me had heard of Bodyline because a text book for her HSC examination in Bombay (now Mumbai) had a chapter on scheming English captain Douglas Jardine's leg theory, later to be known as Bodyline.

So well known is the Bodyline series that my wife who knew nothing of cricket till she met me had heard of Bodyline because a text book for her HSC examination in Bombay (now Mumbai) had a chapter on scheming English captain Douglas Jardine's leg theory, later to be known as Bodyline.

More books are written on Bodyline than on any other cricket topic (except perhaps on Kerry Packer's World Series Cricket of 1977–79). Even a major TV drama series was made of this explosive series by Kennedy Miller Productions in Sydney for Network 10 in 1984. David Frith's *Bodyline Autopsy* (Wisden's book of the year in 2003) and Philip Derriman's *Bodyline – the day England declared war on Australia* (1984) make compulsive reading.

One can write a book on Bodyline and still leave some aspects untouched and unexplained so I will only briefly feature this topic. Why was it conceived, who planned it, who executed it, against whom was it targeted? And more importantly, why was it called 'Bodyline' and who named it Bodyline?

Bodyline became a major international incident involving politicians of two countries, like the underarm incident in the Melbourne one–day international between Australia and New Zealand 49 years later in 1981.

One can write a book on Bodyline and still leave some aspects untouched and unexplained so I will only briefly feature this topic. Why was it conceived, who planned it, who executed it, against whom was it targeted? And more importantly, why was it called 'Bodyline' and who named it Bodyline?

Philip Derriman writes that:

Nothing in sport has caused the feelings of a nation to run so high as the Tests between Australia and England in 1932–33. So great was the indignation of Australians at the bowling methods of the Englishmen that the Australian Prime Minister, Joseph Lyons, and a senior British Cabinet minister, Jimmy Thomas, felt compelled to try to restore good relations between the two countries. The bowling method of the Englishmen came to be called Bodyline, a word which still makes an emotional impact on Australians more than fifty years later. The Bodyline story is the story of an attempt by a fiercely determined captain of England, Douglas Jardine, to overcome the most amazing batsman the world has seen, Don Bradman, and the extraordinary consequences which flowed from the attempt. When film producers came to recreate the story in a television series, they had no need to dramatise it. The drama was already there.

There are many versions to this compelling story. The most plausible one is that the origin of Bodyline grew out of the invincibility of Bradman as a batsman on Australia's tour of England in 1930. In the five Tests the 21 year old, amassed

974 runs (still a record after 82 years) at an average of 139.14, including a century, two double centuries and a triple century.

They were not just tall scores; they were innings by a master batsman who gave bowlers no hope. His 254 in the Lord's Test in 339 minutes with 25 fours is recognised as one of the best innings ever played in Test history. In the following Test at Leeds, he hit 334, then the highest Test score. He smashed 309 runs on the first day; 105 before lunch, 115 between lunch and tea and 89 in the final 90-minute session.

How to curb him in the Ashes in Australia in 1932–33 was England's biggest problem, her priority number one. It is generally believed that Jardine (alone or with others) devised this master plan of transmuting leg theory to Bodyline. Both these terms need definitions and few experts agree on the correct usage. Leg theory is basically bowling to a packed leg–side field in order to put a brake on the batsman's opportunities to score. Bodyline is its evil stepbrother; bowling fast persistent short–pitched deliveries at the batsman's body (hip, shoulder and head) and having a double cluster of fielders on the leg side to take catches off a missed or unintentional hook or pull shot.

Bodyline evolved from various forms of leg–theory bowling. It was being at the top of leg theory's evolutionary tree. 'There were certain external similarities but a vast difference in spirit,' according to Derriman. The Bodyline field consisted of a cordon of five closer fielders from leg–slip to silly mid–on and another two fielders near the long–leg boundary.

Bodyline evolved from various forms of leg–theory bowling. It was being at the top of leg–theory's evolutionary tree. 'There were certain external similarities but a vast difference in spirit,' according to Derriman. The Bodyline field consisted of a cordon of five closer fielders from leg–slip to silly mid–on and another two fielders near the long–leg boundary.

A brainchild of Jardine, the captain of the England team to Australia in 1932–33, assisted by the Nottinghamshire captain, A.W. Carr, this theory was practised against Bradman (among other Australian batsmen) with success where the chief executioner was super–quick Larwood and the venomous Voce. Bradman, who was averaging 112.29 runs an innings in the 19 Tests prior to 1932, could average 'only' 56.57 in four Tests in the Bodyline series. Moreover, of the seven times he was dismissed in this series, Larwood had claimed him four times.

Australian cricketers may have heard alarm bells ringing when the English squad selected four fast bowlers—Larwood, Bill Voce, Gubby Allen and Bill Bowes—for the series. Bradman himself was suspicious as he wrote, 'When the personnel of the English team to Australia in 1932–33 was announced, I saw the possibility of trouble because of the abnormal selection of four fast bowlers.'

Larwood was sure that the pace battery of four was chosen for a purpose. 'There had never been four speed merchants sent to Australia before', he wrote in *The Larwood Story* (1982, coauthor Kevin Perkins), 'Don didn't like the balls rising on his body ... I thought Bradman was a bit frightened of the ball that got up sharply.'

Who coined the word 'Bodyline'? It is believed that cabling a match report to his newspaper from the Sydney Cricket Ground, a journalist Hugh Buggy of Melbourne *Herald*, condensed the phrase 'on the line of the body' to 'Bodyline'. In his autobiography, Larwood wrote that Jardine blamed Buggy for coining the term and bore him a grudge for it.

Ronald Cardwell, the founder of the Australian Cricket Society (NSW branch), informs me:

I am not certain the cable was from the SCG. I thought it was from the MCG. Roy Robinson once told me, 'I went and interviewed Buggy who was a member of the Australian Board of Control. I travelled by tram to his house in Melbourne. Amongst matters discussed he told me, "Larwood bowls along the batsman's body line". When I returned to my newspaper office I wrote a story following my interview. My editor changed the words to read 'Bodyline' and the name was coined'.

David Frith the well-known cricket historian from England and the founder editor of *Wisden Cricket Monthly*, presents another version in his *Bodyline Autopsy* (2002). According to him, Ray Robinson, then with the Melbourne *Herald* [in 1932], had created 'body-line' as an adjective and the unhyphenated version as a noun. It would have featured in a headline earlier than it did but a conservative editor, Syd Deamer, ruled against it.

Frith continues, 'The consensus of credit for the decisive promotion of the word–possibly appropriated rather than invented by him–finally rests with Hugh Buggy, then aged 36, who was writing for the Melbourne *Herald*. The word "Bodyline" appeared in his story on the opening day of the opening Test match.'

But the germ of the word that was to stick originated in the match report of Jack Worrall, formerly an Australian Test batsman and a top Aussie Rules footballer. Frith comments, 'During the Englishmen's early match against an Australian XI at the MCG, Worrall referred to Voce's "half-pitched slingers on the body line". Worrall first used the word "Bodyline" in print on 10 December 1932, just after the opening Test had ended.'

Even after 80 years, variations of the word Bodyline keep cropping up whenever newer controversies make headlines, namely 'Bollyline' during the January 2008 Sydney Test between Australia and India.

Frith succinctly summed up the dramatic series in his *Wisden Cricket Monthly* article in 2002:

Even though there have been over 1300 Test matches in the 70 years since 'Bodyline', it remains the most dramatic Test series of them all. It incorporated the Wild West shoot-out between the young sheriff (Don Bradman from Bowral, NSW) and the narrow-eyed gunslinger (Harold Larwood from Nuncargate, Nottinghamshire). In London and in the cash-strapped dominion of Australia it sparked cloak-and-dagger activity in the cloisters of power-governmental as well as cricketing.

Jack Fingleton who had played in the first three Tests of the Bodyline series and later became a cricket and political journalist, wrote in *Cricket Crisis – Bodyline and other Lines* (1946), 'I do not think there was one single batsman who played in most of those Bodyline games who ever afterwards recaptured his love for cricket.'

[7]
WHY VIZZY SENT
AMARNATH
HOME?

ndia's disastrous tour of England in 1936 was marred by one of cricket's most bizarre controversies when the in-form all-rounder Lala Amarnath was sent home on the eve of the first Test at Lord's on charges of indiscipline by skipper Maharajkumar of Vizianagram, (known as 'Vizzy') and manager R.J. Brittain-Jones.

Both Vizzy and Lala Amarnath were strong unbending characters; one a selfish egoist who sucked up to the British aristocrats to get what he wanted using wealth and charm, the other called an axe an axe come what may. Despite limited talent as a cricketer, Vizzy pushed his way to captain India on the tour of England in 1936.

Amarnath had made a brilliant start to his Test career by becoming the first Indian to score a Test century, against England in Bombay in December 1933. The match had a special meaning for 22-year-old Amarnath as it was the first official home Test for India and it was his Test debut.

Later remembered as the Stormy Petrel of Indian cricket, Amarnath was involved in many controversies. A rebel with a cause he fought the Bigwigs, including the then President of the Indian Cricket Board, Anthony De Mello. As was the catchword of 1930s and 1940s, wherever Amarnath went, could controversies be far behind?

Amarnath was suspended from playing for India in 1949 on accusation of accepting a gift of Rs 5000 to include a player in the Indian XI and 22 other unrelated and unsubstantiated charges. He fought back to prove his innocence and went on to captain India again. Earlier he had led India's first tour of Australia in 1947–48 to replace an injured Vijay Merchant, one of the finest opening batsmen in the world.

In his autobiography *Farewell to Cricket* (1950), Don Bradman wrote:

Throughout the whole of the Australian tour I found Amarnath and [manager] P. Gupta absolutely charming in every respect. They co-operated in all conceivable ways to try and make the games enjoyable, and the most wonderful spirit of camaraderie existed between the Australian and Indian players ... Lala, as he was called, certainly believed in speaking his mind at all times and was not averse to expressing his opinion in regards to a controlling authority or an individual, but in Australia he always did it with the utmost courtesy and tact.

Vizzy's campaign for the captaincy of India bore the stamp of an American presidential campaign. He had journeyed up and down the country gathering votes. Associations that voted for him were promised special consideration when it came to the choice of players for the tour....

Amarnath's performances in State matches were brilliant as, he scored 1162 runs on the tour–the highest ever by an Indian on an Australian tour–at an average of 58, hitting five centuries. His incandescent and unbeaten 228 against Victoria on the MCG came in a crisis when India had lost their first three wickets for no runs. 'Like Shelly's West Wind, Amarnath was the preserver as well as the destroyer,' raved Sujit Mukherjee in *The Romance of Indian Cricket* (1968).

Amarnath later captained India against the West Indies on home turf. Both the series against Australia and the West Indies were lost but Amarnath went on to lead India to triumph against Pakistan in the inaugural series in 1952–53 after charges against him by De Mello were dropped.

Coming back to the controversial 1936 tour—months before this tour Vizzy had used all his political acumen to get the Indian leadership. To quote Mihir Bose from *A History of Indian Cricket* (1990):

Vizzy's campaign for the captaincy of India bore the stamp of an American presidential campaign. He had journeyed up and down the country gathering votes. Associations that voted for him were promised special consideration when it came to the choice of players for the tour ... Vizzy was not only the captain of the side but almost the sole selector.

The manager of the team, Britain–Jones, was the Viceroy of India's nominee and Vizzy's choice. Added Bose, 'This [the 1936 Indian team] was not so much a cricket team as a prince's entourage... He [Vizzy] arrived in England with 36 items of personal luggage and two servants. There was no vice–captain on the tour, no selection committee.'

Bose related another shocking incident involving Vizzy. As Vijay Merchant and Syed Mushtaq Ali walked out to bat in the second innings of the second Test in Manchester in July 1936, Mushtaq revealed to Merchant 'Vizzy has asked me to run you out.' Merchant retorted, 'Just you try!' They had a chuckle although this was no laughing matter. Both hit centuries, Merchant 114 and Mushtaq 112, adding 203 runs. Earlier, Merchant had annoyed Vizzy by suggesting that he should step down as captain.

So we can imagine what a free-speaking spirit like Amarnath went through, climaxed by being sent home in disgrace. In the six weeks leading to the first Test, Amarnath had scored most runs including centuries in both innings against Essex and was also the team's most successful bowler with 32 wickets at 21.00.

Why was a valuable member of the 1936 team, and the best performer on the tour that far, sent home in such a dismissive way? This was Indian cricket's first highly publicised controversy. To quote Boria Majumdar from *Once upon a Furore* (2004):

> The Amarnath–Vizzy affair is evidence of the deep-rooted patrician–plebeian divide that plagued cricket in colonial India. A tussle that dragged on after the conclusion of the 1936 tour, this much reported story of intrigue, corruption and power play had enough in it to be a bestseller.

In the match against Minor Counties, Amarnath was sent in at no.7 with only a few minutes left. He was incensed and on returning to the pavilion he flung his bat and pads down and in choice Punjabi, abused Vizzy. Amarnath was an impetuous young man who suffered no fools and on occasions was his own worst enemy. Previously on the tour he had also argued with Vizzy about field setting.

The match against Minor Counties concluded at 3 p.m. on Friday. At 6 p.m. that day Amarnath was told to pack his bag and catch the boat the next morning. That Friday night, Amarnath pleaded with senior members C.K. Nayudu, Wazir Ali and Mohammad Nissar to talk with Vizzy, manager Brittain–Jones and Lord Willingdon, the Viceroy of India. Amarnath wrote a letter of apology that very night but to no avail. He was soon on the ship *Kaiser-I-Hind* to return to India in disgrace. He was sorely missed as India lost the three–Test series 0–2.

On his return to India, Amarnath met the Nawab of Bhopal and it was almost certain that·he would be sent back to rejoin the team before the second Test in Manchester. But to his acute disappointment he was told that the captain and manager did not want him back. Amarnath was eventually exonerated and went on to captain India with flair, leading India to a series win against Pakistan in 1952–53.

To evenly vaguely understand this unsavoury episode, one has to understand the cloak and dagger politics in Indian cricket in the 1930s; the back–stabbing, the grovelling to the British aristocrats, the power–play. The princes and Maharajahs controlled cricket in India with their wealth and interest in the game but more often to boost their ego. They promoted cricket nationally but they wanted something back for their cash; like inclusion in the national team, preferably as captain.

With the exceptions of princes like K.S. Ranjitsinhji ('Ranji'), his nephew K.S. Duleepsinhji ('Duleep') and the senior Nawab of Pataudi who represented England in Tests with distinction, the majority of the Maharajahs and princes were substandard cricketers.

In *Patrons, Players and the Crowd* (1981), Richard Cashman wrote 'Cricket provided the princes with an outlet of intrigue, pomp and selfish ambition and for conspicuous consumption, and in the process they set back rather than enhanced the development of cricket.'

On the previous tour to England in 1932, where India played their inaugural Test, knives were out much before the tour commenced. Who will captain the side? Colonel C.K. Nayudu was the obvious choice with his flamboyant batting and proven leadership skill but a Maharaja and a prince with little cricketing skills were appointed leaders.

Recognised as a 'six symbol', C.K. would have been the first choice in today's Twenty20 cricket. He is remembered for hitting MCC's Test class bowlers Maurice Tate and J Mercer for 11 sixes in his 153 in 116 minutes in Bombay in 1926, a world record then. According to the great English writer Neville Cardus in 1932, 'Nayudu is lithe, wristy and volatile, for each of his strokes you get the impression of a new–born energy.'

An army disciplinarian, Nayudu was a leader of men. Yet, lesser men were preferred to captain India for the tour to England in 1932. The Maharajah of Porbander (who had reportedly more Rolls–Royce cars than scored runs) and prince G.S. Ganshyamsinhji were appointed captain and vice-captain for that tour. But with a batting average of 0.66 on the tour (highest score 2) in earlier matches, Porbander realised his limitations and handed over the captaincy to C.K. Nayudu, Indian cricket's first super star, in the only Test at Lord's.

Not so for Vizzy, the Maharajkumar of Vizianagram, on the 1936 tour. He was determined to lead India come what may. He did not get on with C.K. Nayudu and ordered Amarnath and others not to mix socially with him. Amarnath agreed to keep his skipper happy. But even then 24-year-old Amarnath had a fiery streak and was annoyed when Vizzy refused to give him the field setting he wanted. Any argument meant he was sent to deep outfield even when he had a foot injury.

My uncle, Kharshed R. Meher-Homji (1911-1981), was on that tour as a wicketkeeper and told me this story in 1958 when I was a student. 'Vizzy, a useless batsman, would pad up when a spinner was operating', he reminisced:

> But if a speedster was bowling when a wicket fell, he would ask someone else to pad up and go out to bat. Team members would keep quiet so as not to offend the selfish and autocratic skipper. But one day, Lala [Amarnath] could take it no longer and told him off. Soon he was in the boat Kaiser-I-Hind for insubordination on a one-way ticket.

'Insubordination, my foot', raged my uncle, 22 years after the incident. Many versions are given for the Amarnath sacking but the above explanation seems most plausible. Later, it was a great pleasure to be introduced to Lala by uncle Kharshed and we had a longish chat including about the Vizzy confrontation, peppered with some choice and red-hot Punjabi expletives.

The Beaumont Committee appointed to deliberate on the 1936 controversy found Amarnath guilty and supported Vizzy's and Brittain-Jones' action in sending back Amarnath on grounds of indiscipline and misbehaviour. But a fighter for justice, Amarnath returned to Indian cricket as an all-rounder and a captain, his reputation intact.

LALA AMARNATH PASSED AWAY IN 2000 aged 88. Two of his sons, Surinder and Mohinder, played Test cricket for India, left-handed Surinder emulating his dad by scoring a century on his Test debut. All-rounder Mohinder was one of the heroes of India's World Cup victory in 1983 and later became a national selector.

[8]
MANKADED
DOWN UNDER

L ala Amarnath figures once again in this chapter but not as a main actor but rather as an 'extra'. He captained India on this inaugural tour of Australia in 1947–48, during a period of political importance and turmoil for India. A few months before this tour, India had gained independence on 15 August 1947 and as the tour was progressing, Mahatma Gandhi—the great apostle of peace— was assassinated on 30 January 1948, two days after the fourth Test in Adelaide concluded.

Australia was then at her strongest with master batsmen Don Bradman, Lindsay Hassett, Bill Brown, Sid Barnes, Arthur Morris and Neil Harvey, all-time great all-rounder Keith Miller, the pace trio of Ray Lindwall, Miller and Bill Johnston, the spin of Ian Johnson, Ernie Toshack and Doug Ring with the legendary Don Tallon behind the stumps. They were described as 'invincible' when touring England in 1948.

Australia was then at her strongest with master batsmen Don Bradman, Lindsay Hassett, Bill Brown, Sid Barnes, Arthur Morris and Neil Harvey, all-time great all-rounder Keith Miller, the pace trio of Ray Lindwall, Miller and Bill Johnston, the spin of Ian Johnson, Ernie Toshack and Doug Ring with the legendary Don Tallon behind the stumps.

On the other hand, India had a weakened team as they missed four stars; world-class opening batsman Vijay Merchant (dubbed the 'Bradman of India') due to injury, the dashing hitter Mushtaq Ali, all-rounder Abdul Hafeez Kardar and fast-medium bowler Fazal Mahmood (who later shone out as a world-class swing bowler and called the 'Alec Bedser of Pakistan') because of an unsettled political situation due to the partition of Pakistan from India and the prolific and stylish batsman Rusi Modi who had a nervous breakdown.

In Merchant's absence Amarnath captained India. Although he failed dismally in the Tests, averaging only 14, his performances in State matches were so brilliant that, according to former Test cricketer Arthur Mailey, people thronged to the grounds to see Amarnath bat and not Bradman. He played a majestic innings of 228 against Victoria on the MCG. He had come in to bat with India in deep trouble at three down for no runs and played an innings 'old–timers' still remember with awe. He scored 1162 runs on the tour–the highest ever by an Indian on an Australian tour–at an average of 58, hitting five centuries (144, 228 not out, 172 not out, 171 and 135).

It was a tour to cherish for vice–captain Vijay Hazare, a classical batsman and a crisis specialist. Against the fury of Lindwall and Miller in the Adelaide Test, seven Indians failed to score and India lost by an innings but the heroic Hazare, described as a Rock of Gibraltar, made 116 and 145.

Wrote Bradman in his autobiography *Farewell to Cricket* (1950), 'I look back on the season with him [Amarnath] as my opposite number as one of my most pleasant cricket years ... In the batting line, Amarnath and Hazare were outstanding. They were fit to be classed in any company.'

However, this chapter is on leg–spinning all–rounder Vinoo Mankad so let's zoom down to him and how the word 'Mankaded' was coined. On the Australian tour, Mankad shone out with bat and ball. He hit centuries in the third and fifth Tests in Melbourne. Praising his bowling, Jack Fingleton described Mankad as 'the best of his kind since Hedley Verity'.

On this tour, Mankad was involved in an incident that gave him some unjustified notoriety. When bowling against the Australian XI he noticed Bill Brown at the bowler's end leaving the crease before he delivered the ball. He warned Brown once but next time ran him out by whipping off the bails in the act of delivering the ball. Mankad did the same in the Sydney Test and a new cricket phrase was coined: 'to be mankaded'.

Many Australian critics labelled this as an act of unsportsmanship. Bradman defended Mankad in his autobiography *Farewell to Cricket*:

In some quarters Mankad's sportsmanship was questioned. For the life of me I cannot understand why. The laws of cricket make it quite clear that the non–striker must keep within his ground until the ball has been delivered. If not, why is the provision there which enables the bowler to run him out? By backing up too far or too early, the non–striker is very obviously gaining an unfair advantage. On numerous occasions he may avoid getting run out at the opposite end by gaining this false start.

Bradman added that it would be difficult for a fast bowler to do what Mankad did but a spinner has a chance. He added, 'Mankad was an ideal type, and he was so scrupulously fair that he first of all warned Brown before taking any action. There was absolutely no feeling in the matter as far as we were concerned, for we considered it quite a legitimate part of the game.'

When the team departed for India, the Don presented him with an autographed photograph with the words 'Well played, Mankad' inscribed on it. Mankad treasured this until he died in 1978.

But the word 'mankaded' has stuck and crops up in cricket reports after 65 years. By introducing new rules, a bowler could not 'mankad' a batsman out till 2011. But later that year the ICC changed its playing conditions to allow a bowler to 'mankad' a batsman any time before he had completed the usual delivery swing of his arm. Prior to that, the ICC rule stated that a bowler could only attempt to run out a batsman backing up at the non–striker's end if he did so before he had entered his delivery stride.

The term 'mankaded' resurfaced in Sri Lanka's match against India at Brisbane on 21 February 2012. Sri Lankan non–striking batsman Lahiru Thirimanne left the crease before India's off–spinner Ravichandra Ashwin delivered the ball. So Ashwin broke the stumps and looked at the umpire for a run-out decision. By the new Law the non–striker Thirimanne was out but to avoid future controversy, the two on–field umpires consulted India's skipper Virender Sehwag whether he would like to withdraw the appeal, which he did.

Thirimanne survived. He was 44 then and Sri Lanka 4 for196. He went on to top score with 62 as his country reached 289 and won. A question: would Sri Lanka have reached this target if Thirimanne was given out as per the rules in the 40th over with Sri Lanka needing 93 runs with five wickets left in ten overs? Defiantly, Thirimanne continued leaving the crease at the bowler's end, which was against both the revised law of the game and its spirit as well.

FORMER TEST CRICKETER JACK FINGLETON NARRATED an entertaining anecdote on his contemporary Bill 'Tiger' O'Reilly in his book *Fingleton on Cricket* (1971). They were discussing West Indian quickie Charlie Griffiths 'mankading' Australia's Ian Redpath during the 1969 Adelaide Test. O'Reilly felt that the onus was on Redpath to see that he did not leave the crease before the ball was bowled. Fingleton then asked him, as to how many batsmen he had 'mankaded'. Without hesitation, O'Reilly shot back, 'I never found that the batsmen were overkeen to get to the other end to face me!'

THE FLAMING
BOMBAY TEST

was actually *there*, sitting along with the rioters and arsonists in the East Stand of Brabourne Stadium, Bombay (now Mumbai), keeping my mouth shut lest I might go up in smoke. It was the scariest moment of my life as I watched the notorious Bombay Test between Australia and India in November 1969. For once in my life, I felt ashamed to be an Indian. The behaviour of the crowd in the East Stand was unforgivable.

They were not so much against Australians as against their own umpire Shambu Pan who had declared Indian batsman Srinivasan Venkataraghavan out, caught behind. It was a shocking decision, which would have passed unnoticed but the radio commentator Devraj Puri kept stressing that the bat was nowhere near the ball. As many spectators had transistor radios—a new fad then—held near their ears, their resentment turned into anger and then rage. Even sensible watchers on my left and right turned from Dr Jekyll to Mr Hyde within minutes.

The decision to give Venkat out was a shocker as wicketkeeper Brian Taber who held that catch off Alan Connolly recently told me in Sydney. 'We had appealed half in jest and were surprised to see the umpire's finger go up!' But the crowd saw no humour in it. They set fire to the chairs and threw the flaming chairs on the ground. They also expected Australia's skipper Bill Lawry to recall Venkat as the great West Indies captain Garry Sobers had done on the same ground two years earlier.

This was the first Test of the series and I almost did not see it. Tickets went for sale a few days before the Test and I joined almost a mile-long queue outside Brabourne Stadium at 3.30 a.m. Windows opened at 9 a.m. but I missed out and was devastated. The scalpers were selling a ticket for Rs 2600 (about A$40), a huge amount then. But my friend Anandji Dossa, a well-known cricket statistician, somehow managed to get for me a ticket in the East Stand, notorious for crowd disturbances.

Controversy started before the match. The omission of Venkataraghavan from the team had caused such a public outcry that Subrata Guha agreed to stand down from the selected team. Australia took a modest 74 runs first innings lead, thanks to Keith Stackpole hitting a hundred. He became the first Australian after Don Bradman to score a century in his first Test against India.

The match was then evenly poised but the Indian batsmen collapsed in a heap in the second innings and were seven down for 89, only 15 runs ahead. Ajit Wadekar and Venkat (who both went on to captain India) were staging a mini recovery by adding 25 runs when the umpiring howler almost ended the match on the fourth day.

As Ray Robinson colourfully wrote in *The Wildest Tests* (1979), 'Before you could say Venkataraghavan, mob fury exploded in scenes unprecedented in the city's cricket history.'

Controversy started before the match. The omission of Venkataraghavan from the team had caused such a public outcry that Subrata Guha agreed to stand down from the selected team. Australia took a modest 74 runs first innings lead, thanks to Keith Stackpole hitting a hundred.

The Test resumed without Venkat, as new batsman E.A.S. Prasanna joined Wadekar. As Connolly bowled to Prasanna, enraged spectators set fire to hessian around the tennis courts behind the East Stand. Others heaped hundreds of chairs on fire and set parts of the North Stand and Bombay Cricket Association Stand alight. Awning coverings were soon ablaze. Smoke blew over the field and with 30 minutes to go it was difficult to watch the game.

Yet, the match continued as Lawry refused to take his team in as he wanted to win the game come smoke or flying burning chairs! G.K. Menon, the columnist for *Indian Express*, rushed to the middle and said, 'Stop the game. We can't see it as smoke is getting in our eyes.' Yet Lawry was unmoved and barked a reproof at the columnist who had no right to enter the playing arena. Menon gave back what he received from Lawry.

It got uglier as the East Standers got rowdier. Bottles with broken necks were thrown on the ground. Moving out of danger, off-spinner Ashley Mallett stood near gully. When Lawry asked what he was doing there, he responded, 'Just have a look at what's happening down there', pointing at the troubled spot littered with broken bottles. But Lawry refused to return to the pavilion, a Test victory was more important to him than team safety.

Just then an angry mass of spectators flung their weight against the wire-mesh barricade in front of the East Stand. Terrified, I wanted to go home but was blocked by men with broken bottles. Two stands were cleared by the riot police and the fires were eventually put out.

K.N. Prabhu, the respected sports editor of *The Times of India*, called it a day of infamy for Indian cricket and supported Lawry's stand. He wrote in the next day's paper:

It is to the credit of Lawry and his men that, among din and uproar, they stood their ground and carried on with the game as best as they could. And Wadekar, too, held his ground, phlegmatic and unperturbed by the dismal turn of events on and off the field ... The major casuality was the fair name of Indian cricket.

Another Indian journalist Rajan Bala described the Venkat dismissal in his book *Kiwis and Kangaroos — India 1969* (1970):

From the press box which is situated at a highly disadvantageous extra–cover it looked for a moment that Stackpole at second slip had taken the catch. What led credence to the view was the fact that wicketkeeper Brian Taber did not appeal. However, with a combination of the comments of the radio commentator and the majority in the press box the scorers on a consensus recorded that the wicketkeeper had taken the catch. The explanation of the doubt was that Taber after taking ball had passed it on to Stackpole in the course of things. And a half smothered appeal from the bowler (a possibility when there has been a near miss) caused umpire Pan to implacably raise the fatal finger.

Venkataraghavan who was in the process of settling down for the next delivery was thunderstruck and evidently displeased when he was informed that he was given out. He gave Pan an angry look ... and stalked off. Wadekar, the non–striker, spoke to Pan, a completely unnecessary action, which only did its part in aggravating the situation as the crowd began registering their loud and angry disapproval ...

It was almost like the ancient Roman arena as the crowd demanded Bill Lawry's and Pan's blood. The steady roar of 'we want Venkat' slowly became 'shame, shame Lawry' and finally degenerated into 'Australian team go home.

It was disgusting, alarming and horrifying. On police advice, Lawry's men stayed on the field for twenty minutes as the riot squad tried to clear intruders from the members' reserve. Watchmen carrying mesh shields escorted the players to

Just then an angry mass of spectators flung their weight against the wire–mesh barricade in front of the East Stand. Terrified, I wanted to go home but was blocked by men with broken bottles. Two stands were cleared by the riot police and the fires were eventually put out.

the clubhouse as Stackpole and Mallett carried stumps, just in case. In a final paroxysm of frenzy, bottles broke every window of the visitors' dressing rooms so the Australian team was hurriedly hidden in the Cricket Club of India's shower and toilet blocks.

Who was to blame for this violence? First and last the rowdy crowd whose behaviour was indefensible. Umpires make mistakes and Pan made a big one. Only a slim minority of captains would recall a batsman back when given out wrongly and Lawry never claimed himself to be a Sobers. The commentator Devraj Puri who said what he saw was perhaps responsible for the ugly consequences but he was only doing his job to call a match accurately.

But to remain on the field when the riot erupted was unwise. In my opinion it was foolhardy, since in extreme cases, strategic retreat is no cowardice but wisdom.

Australia won the Test by eight wickets and went on to claim the series 3–1. But they were whitewashed 0–4 in South Africa a few months later and Lawry lost his captaincy to Ian Chappell in early 1971. It seemed poetic, almost ironic, that off–spinner Venkataraghavan became a well-respected umpire after he retired from Test cricket.

When I interviewed Mallett recently, he had an interesting take on the incident:

Venkat was given out caught behind off Alan Connolly. I was at short third man and clearly heard a noise, but after talking to wicketkeeper Brian Taber it appeared the 'noise' was a creaking bat handle.

I believe the riot was a result of a number of factors. Firstly, people who had saved up for a year for the Test match found that their booked seats were 'taken'. There were apparently a lot of forged tickets. When Venkat was given out 'wrongly' according to the radio commentators, frustrated spectators set alight the stacked deck chairs, people tried to push the outer fence over, cars were set alight outside Brabourne Stadium and a nearby tennis club was torched.

Because of the pall of smoke wafting over the ground the scorer rushed up to Lawry and said he 'couldn't see and I'm going home'. So the main man of the radio became the 'new' scorer. I don't think Lawry should have recalled Venkat. Those were the days before video reviews and we simply had to rely totally on the umpire's decision. There certainly was a big noise, which sounded like bat touching ball, but a replay would have shown Venkat had missed the ball by a fair margin.

The radio commentator apparently called Lawry 'a cheat' over this dismissal and there were many people in the outer clinging to their transistor radios, a free gift for those practising birth control. In the 1969 Indian Telephone Directory there was a big ad: 'HAVE TWO AND THAT WILL DO'. The government decreed that if a bloke had two children and was prepared to have a vasectomy (presumably to halt the population explosion) it would donate the person a brand new transistor radio. The scheme may have helped that riot of 1969 but not a halt in population growth. Over the past 40 years India's population has increased alarmingly.

And this is Ian Chappell's version of the burning of Brabourne Stadium Test when I interviewed him for this book:

The incident started when Venkat was given out (incorrectly in the opinion of at least two of the fielders behind the wicket) caught behind off Alan Connolly. We were later told the radio announcer said Venkat wasn't out and Bill Lawry should recall him. This apparently set the crowd off.

It started with some rubbish being thrown on the Shamianas at the opposite end to the pavilion and then a few chairs and finally someone set fire to the pile. Over on the right (looking from the pavilion) the crowd began throwing bottles onto the field and Doug Walters threatened to throw one at them if they hit him.

Eventually the police came onto the field and started throwing the bottles back into the crowd and they were exploding on the concrete steps. This forced the crowd up the stand to the point where some apparently jumped off the back to avoid being hit by flying glass and bottles. By this stage a fire had also been started in that area with the crowd burning the wooden seats.

Meanwhile, the fire had really taken hold at the end of the ground and black smoke was billowing everywhere. Two guys ran onto the field and I thought it was the start of the crowd storming the field as they had been pushing and shaking the fence that kept the fans off the field. However, it was the official scorers who came out to tell the umpires they had to stop the game because they couldn't see what was going on.

Bill told the scorers to get off the field so we could continue the game. At the end of the day's play John Gleeson was hit with a chair that had been thrown from the upper level of the pavilion and apparently he stumbled and fell. Fortunately, manager Fred Bennett was walking out to meet the team and he saw Gleeson go down because John was at the rear of the players coming off the field and no one else saw what happened.

After play a few of the Australian team went into the Indian dressing room and it was like an emergency room at the hospital; members of the crowd had been treated in there and quite a few were walking around with bloody bandages on their body.

Dougie humour

DOUG WALTERS SEES HUMOUR IN EVERY situation, even during a riot. Ashley Mallett recalls, 'After play on the fourth stressful day, our manager Fred Bennett rushed into a room Doug Walters had barricaded—along with a bathtub of iced beer.

'Fellas, there are 10 000 people outside the foyer baying for Lawry's blood. What do we do?'

Walters waited for the right moment and said coolly, 'Fred, give 'em Bill Lawry and let's get on with the drinking!'

Single-minded Lawry

'TO SAY BILL "PHANTOM" LAWRY WAS a tough captain was to understate the case', wrote Ian Chappell in *Chappelli Laughs Again* (1981). A lesser captain would have buckled to the pressure of the 1969 Mumbai Test riot but Chappell wondered whether Lawry realised that there was a riot on, so focused he was on the game as he put the chants of 'Kill Lawry, kill Lawry' in his subconscious. When Chappell suggested to him the safest way to exit from the rioters he turned a deaf ear. When Chappell persisted, 'What do you think, Phantom?' He replied, 'Christ, we need a wicket bad.'

[10]
SNOW STORM
LEADS TO SCG
WALK-OFF

I t seems weird, almost a déjà vu. The last Test I saw in India before I migrated to Australia was the infamous Bombay (now Mumbai) Test between Australia and India in November 1969. The second Test I saw in Australia was another bad-tempered match. It was the final Test of the Ashes series in Sydney in February 1971 where England's captain Ray Illingworth ('Illy') took his team in for a protest against beer can throwing by some spectators from the Hill area.

The captains' decisions in these Tests 15 months apart were contradictory to the extreme; Lawry not taking his team in when he should have and Illingworth taking his team in when he should not have. Let's revisit the 1971 Sydney Test.

A few days before the Test there were headlines because of the dropping of Lawry as both captain and player in the match. He was replaced by Ian Chappell, who took the reins as Australia's skipper.

The 1970–71 Ashes series was dominated by John Snow, the aggressive fast bowler from England. In his engrossing book *The Wildest Tests* (1979), Ray Robinson described Snow as 'a swordfish among salmon; to most of Australia's batsmen a more apt simile might be like a piranha among perch, ready to tear strips off their already worn confidence'.

He not only bowled short–pitched balls bouncing high, he also had a short temper and tended to explode when an umpire warned him for intimidating bowling. He was warned three times in earlier Tests by umpires. In the second innings of the Perth Test when no–nonsense Australian umpire Lou Rowan (also a police detective) asked Snow to 'watch it', he brusquely asked 'what for?' After the second warning in Perth, Rowan approached captain Illingworth, who responded, 'They're not bouncers'. Rowan replied sarcastically, 'Somebody's bowling these from this end and it's not me.'

Arguments got hotter as the series progressed and it was at fever pitch in the seventh Test at the SCG. Lou Rowan in his autobiography *The Umpire's Story* (1973) starts off with a 'bouncer' himself:

Here we had an event as potentially dangerous to the traditions and aspirations of international cricket as the notorious Bodyline series of England–Australia Tests of 1932–33.
For at the centre of the whole affair, we had two men of extreme strong but cantankerous personality, Ray Illingworth and John Snow, the Vicar's son–both of

them cricketers of high skill, both of them pugnaciously eager to win, both of them in need of careful handling for the game's sake when a noisy crowd irritated them, such as in Sydney.

I had migrated to Australia only a few months ago and to watch this explosive Sydney Test made me feel at home, having witnessed violent crowd behaviour in Mumbai and Calcutta (now Kolkata). But the sight of a spectator having an altercation with a player on the boundary line and beer cans flying onto the ground was a frightening experience even for me. The opening day was eventful as England, sent in to bat by the debutant captain Ian Chappell, was bowled out for 184— spinners Terry Jenner and Kerry O'Keeffe took three wickets each.

The drama started after tea on the second day, 13 February. Snow had the Australian batsmen in trouble with his pace like fire and perfectly pitched bouncers. They were 7 for 178 when spinner and tailender Jenner walked in to bat to join the majestic batsman Greg Chappell. Snow gave Jenner the full treatment, two short deliveries as Illingworth brought the fielders closer. The next ball from Snow was a screamingly fast bouncer that hit Jenner on the back of his neck. I remember the crack on the back of Jenner's head even after 40 years. He was bleeding profusely from the head wound and was knocked out like a boxer. Rowan called it a 'dead ball' immediately.

As Jenner was helped out from the field and Dennis Lillee got ready to face Snow, Rowan told the aggressive bowler in a moderate tone to ease up on those short deliveries. Rowan colourfully narrates in *The Umpire's Story*, 'Snow stopped in his tracks and, in a most belligerent attitude said, "What rot! That's the only —— bouncer I've bowled. It's not my fault he got hit." '

According to Rowan, Illingworth was incensed that Snow had received a caution from him, and said in a raised voice: 'You can't — well caution him — hell ... I'll report you.' Then Snow made an outburst saying, 'You're a — cheat.'

To be unbiased, I must add that during England's first innings a day before, debutant Tony Dell and Lillee had bowled their fair share of short-pitched deliveries as had Lillee and Alan 'Froggy' Thomson in the previous Tests in this series. To quote Robinson from *The Wildest Tests*:

> Watching through binoculars [in the fifth Test in Melbourne] I wondered would the umpire walk across to intercept 'Froggy' [Thomson] with an admonition. I saw no sign of this, nor anything being said to the bowler when a fifth bouncer struck the ducking [English batsman Brian] Luckhurst near a shoulder blade.

But when Snow bowled four bouncers in an over to Doug Walters, umpire Max O'Connell said, 'That's enough'. Running from point, Illingworth protested to O'Connell about this double standard—Snow being warned for fewer bouncers than 'Froggy' Thomson had in one over in the first innings in Melbourne.

Thus there was animosity before the seventh Test commenced in Sydney. Greg Chappell was at the other end when the Snow, Jenner, Illingworth, Rowan drama took place. To quote him from his autobiography *Fierce Focus* (2011):

> Illy [Illingworth], Snowy and the umpire Lou Rowan were at each other that afternoon, as they had been all series. In England's tour match in Queensland, Lou, a Queensland copper, had been no-balling Snowy. He started again in Sydney. But Snowy was like a metronome. He landed in the same spot every time and Illy couldn't believe he was no-balling ... I watched Snowy's foot and Lou called him. But it wasn't a no-ball; I saw it.
> Snowy tended to bowl short, and now he was in a temper. Up the other end, T.J. [Terry Jenner] was terrified, expecting a bouncer every ball... Terry made up his mind that the bouncer was coming, and he was ducking even before Snowy had let go off the ball.

The rest has become part of Aussie history.

The crowd noise rose to a tumult when Jenner was knocked down and apparently bleeding off a Snow bouncer. They got angrier as Snow, Illingworth and Rowan exchanged words. At the end of the over Illingworth sent Snow to the fine–leg fence. Was this a deliberately provocative action by the England skipper as the Hill area was noted for its wild behaviour?

Talk of asking for trouble. Soon Snow became involved in an altercation with an angry spectator. Things became nastier as fielders rushed to the trouble spot. Empty beer cans were thrown on the ground. It was absolute bedlam! Illingworth told his players for a sit–down, which angered the crowd even more. With the crowd roaring for cricketing action and more empty beer cans being hurled on the ground, Illingworth led his team from the field, although some of his team members were hesitant.

Rowan continues the story, 'Without even so much as a word or a gesture to either umpire, he began the walk–off which headed England, the MCC, even cricket itself, towards what might develop into the blackest moment in the sport's history.'

The umpires, Rowan and Tom Brooks, could have declared the game closed with Australia winning by forfeit. But they did not want to act in a hurry and regret it later. They gave England a chance to resume the play because the consequences would have been grave for not only the game of cricket but for relations between the two mighty nations. They also felt that if the game was abandoned, a violent riot would replace the cacophonic noise.

The umpires accompanied by the managers of Australian and English teams—Alan Barnes and David Clark—approached Illingworth in the visitors' Dressing Room and asked him, 'Do you propose to resume the game or to forfeit?'

Illingworth asked for police protection. Rowan told him that the ground will be cleared of beer cans and other litter. 'You will then resume or forfeit the game.' England decided to resume and the crowd showed full appreciation of the visitors' return to the field. A major crisis

But when Snow bowled four bouncers in an over to Doug Walters, umpire Max O'Connell said, 'That's enough'. Running from point, Illingworth protested to O'Connell about this double standard–Snow being warned for fewer bouncers than 'Froggy' Thomson had in one over in the first innings in Melbourne.

was averted, thanks to umpires behaving firmly but sensibly.

There was a similar incidence in the forfeited Oval Test between England and

APART FROM BEING A LEGENDARY FAST bowler, John Snow was also a poet. His poem *Contrasts* ends:

On the treadmill rolls
As the body mindless bowls
Down paths
And the wheel which turns
Is turning much faster than before.

Philip Derriman, historian and author of many cricket books and a former Sydney Morning Herald columnist, did an excellent search to trace the spectator who had grabbed John Snow near the Hill area after the incident involving Terry Jenner. To quote him from his new book *100 TESTS: A Century of Test Match Cricket at the Sydney Cricket Ground*:

The story of the John Snow incident does have a sequel, and it concerns the man in the white towelling hat. In the 1980s, when the affair was still reasonably fresh in everyone's memory, I made several attempts to find out who the unidentified man was. I spoke to various cricket writers and ground officials who were at the SCG that day but they were not able to help. So much had happened so quickly after Snow was grabbed by the spectator that none of the cricket writers on duty that day had time to try to track down the spectator who did the grabbing. He had simply melted back into the crowd.

In the late 1990s, nearly 30 years after the event, I made a last-ditch attempt to identify him by enlisting the help of the ABC Radio broadcaster Ian McNamara, who was kind enough to mention on his Sunday morning program a week or two later that I was keen to contact the man in the white towelling hat, assuming he was still alive. The broadcast was heard by a businessman in Tasmania named Jim Morrison, who, as it turned out, knew all about the man in question, for he happened to be the man's son-in-law.

It then emerged that the man in the white towelling hat had been a 53-year old Tasmanian named Trevor Guy, who had moved to Sydney a few years earlier and lived at Sylvania Waters. He had gone to the cricket that day with a group of men he worked with at AWA in Sydney, plus a few friends and relatives. Guy was a big man who held strong views on matters that interested him, including sport, but by all accounts he was far from aggressive by nature. Someone who knew him described him as a gentle giant. So the others in the group were surprised when, on a sudden impulse, Guy got up and walked down to the fence to confront Snow. It seems he had been fuming about the ball that hit Jenner, and he wanted to tell Snow what he thought of fast bowlers who bowled bumpers at tail-enders. He grabbed Snow, it seems, not as an act of violence but simply to make sure Snow heard what he had to say. What happened next, is history.

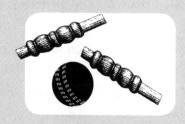

11

WORLD SERIES
CRICKET
REVOLUTION

Wor ld Series Cricket was the biggest game changer in cricket history; bigger than Bodyline, bigger than Ben Hur. No golden chariots, no jousting between knights in silver armour on horsebacks but top-class cricketers demanding proper payment for their days in the sun. And their emancipator was none other than Australian television mogul and billionaire Kerry Packer.

It was *Quo Vadis* revisited in 1977. You cannot call yourself a cricket follower if you do not remember Packer cricket or as the late Bill O'Reilly (regarded as one of the greatest bowlers of all time) would call it the 'Packer circus'. Books have been written on the controversy that divided not only Australians but the cricket world. Establishment against Rebels headlines filled newspapers from 1977 to 1979. Peter McFarline's *A Game Divided* (1977) and Gideon Haigh's *Cricket War. The Inside Story of Kerry Packer's World Series* (1993) go into minute details as to how the idea was conceived, developed in secrecy and revealed to a stunned audience.

World Series changed cricket as never before and never since. One of the highlights of my career was watching the exhilarating Centenary Test of March 1977 staged in Melbourne, played exactly 100 years after the inaugural Test on the same venue and incredibly won again by Australia by the identical margin of 45 runs. It could not get any better.

> *Books have been written on the controversy that divided not only Australians but the cricket world. Establishment against Rebels headlines filled newspapers from 1977 to 1979. Peter McFarline's* A Game Divided *(1977) and Gideon Haigh's* Cricket War.

The brainchild of Hans Ebeling (Australian Test bowler who had made his debut in The Oval Test of 1934), this celebration match, for which the Ashes were not at stake, attracted the largest collection of international cricketers—past and current—in history. Not to forget Queen Elizabeth and the Duke of Edinburgh. There were many heroes in this memorable match, Dennis Lillee taking 11 wickets (6 for 26 and 5 for 139), Rod Marsh becoming the first Australian wicketkeeper to score a Test century and England's eccentric batsman Derek Randall recording the second-highest innings by a debutant in a Test against Australia. England's total of 417 was the highest in the second innings in a series against Australia.

The sublime moment for me was when Marsh recalled Randall. At 161, umpire Tom Brooks had given him out, caught behind. Immediately, Marsh intimated to the umpire that he had dropped the catch and Randall was called back. It was cricket played in the best spirit and the future of Test cricket was at its rosiest. Reg Hayter in *Wisden* 1978 suggested, tongue–in–cheek, that the inspiration behind this Centenary Test, Hans Ebeling, be christened Hans Anderson Ebeling.

However, two months later, the cricket followers reeled when it was revealed that Sydney television magnate Kerry Packer had contracted 35 of the best cricketers to take part in a private, professional series during the next Australian season. To quote Gideon Haigh from *The Oxford Companion to Australian Cricket* (1996):

> Responses uniformly scornful and derisive did not anticipate the way in which 'the Packer Circus' would alter the fabric of the game. Within three years, cricket in Australia would be swept from its traditional semi–amateur roots into a professionalised spectacle in which television was a cornerstone.

There were many reasons behind the creation of World Series Cricket (WSC). Packer wanted to televise all Test matches in Australia on his TCN 9, Sydney. His Consolidated Press's bid for Test telecast rights were rebuffed in 1976 by the Australian Cricket Board (ACB). In retrospect, one feels that had ACB negotiated with Packer, the outcome would have been entirely different.

Then of course adequate payment to players was another major issue. Megastars, such as Dennis Lillee, Ian and Greg Chappell, Doug Walters, Jeff Thomson, Rod Marsh had cult followings wherever cricket was played. They brought in crowds of huge numbers to increase gate money for ACB. And these players who had done so much for Australian cricket were paid poorly as compared to say footballers, boxers, Rugby League and tennis players. The cricketers' revolt was on the cards but the ACB looked the other way.

Packer, an astute businessman, combined the two burning issues stated above and WSC was born. With cool heads, the so–called revolution could have been avoided. Packer offered cricketers bigger pay cheques (which they deserved) and could televise high-quality matches between the best players in the world for his Channel 9.

In December 1976, four months before the Centenary Test, Packer authorised Dennis Lillee's managers John Cornell and Austin Robertson to assemble a troupe of international cricketers. Lillee was the first signatory. He was to receive a A$105 000 three-season package in contrast to his A$400 Test match base fee. The agents secretly signed in 18 Australians, including 13 members of the 1977 squad that toured England seven months later. They were Dennis Lillee, Ian Chappell, Greg Chappell, Rod Marsh, Doug Walters, Jeff Thomson, Len Pascoe, Ray Bright, Kerry O'Keeffe, Ian Davis, David Hookes, Rick McCosker, Richie Robinson, Max Walker, Mick Malone, Ian Redpath, Ross Edwards and Gary Gilmour.

'In March 1977, Packer himself obtained the signature of England's South Africa-born captain Tony Greig who volunteered to become a recruiting agent for foreign cricketers', to quote Haigh. And to think that Greig was captaining England in the most entertaining and historic Centenary Test when no one outside the group had an inclination of what was happening off field where walls had no ears.

At the 2012 MCC Spirit of Cricket Cowdrey Lecture at Lord's, London, in June 2012, Greig explained why he joined WSC. 'A quote from the transcript of my meeting with Kerry Packer, five days after the Centenary Test on 22 March 1977, gives the best insight into how I felt at the time:

> Kerry, money is not my major concern. I'm nearly 31 years old. I'm probably two or three Test failures from being dropped from the England team. Ian Botham is going to be a great player and there won't be room in the England Test side for both of us. England captains, such as Tony Lewis, Brian Close, Colin Cowdrey, Ray Illingworth and Mike Denness all lost the captaincy long before they expected. I won't be any different. I don't want to finish up in a mundane job when they drop me. I'm not trained to do anything. I went straight from school to playing for Sussex. I am at the stage in my life where my family's future is more important than anything else. If you guarantee me a job for life working for your organisation I will sign.

And he not only signed for WSC but recruited players from around the world.

He joined agent Robertson in Trinidad where the West Indies were playing a Test match against Pakistan in April. Eight of the best players were signed in secretly. They were captain Clive Lloyd, Viv Richards, Andy Roberts and Michael Holding from West Indies and skipper Mushtaq Mohammad, Majid Khan, Imran Khan and Asif Iqbal from Pakistan. Greig then approached cricketers from South Africa (Graeme Pollock, Mike Procter, Barry Richards, Eddie Barlow and Denys Hobson who were starved of international cricket) and England's John Snow, Alan Knott and Derek Underwood.

In all, 35 players were recruited worldwide when the plans were revealed prematurely by Australian journalists Peter McFarline and Alan Shiell on 9 May 1977. 'The planning of the Packer troupe and the series of so-called Supertests in Australia during the summer of 1977–78 was undoubtedly the best kept secret in sporting history', wrote McFarline in *A Game Divided* (1977):

> I first learnt about it, in general terms, in September 1976 and on 2 October, wrote an article in *the Age* outlining Channel 9's attempt to run a series of televised games, involving some of the world's best players. The story was quickly, and effectively, denied by Channel 9's Melbourne office.

But it became a reality when the Supertests, with the world's finest cricketers, competed with the thrillingly entertaining Test series between the traditional Australian team and India. Australia was captained by Bob Simpson who had retired from the Test arena a decade ago and India was led by the colourfully turbaned Bishan Singh Bedi. Those from the Establishment were highly critical of Packer's plan to take over international cricket. He had crucial meetings with the International Cricket Council (ICC) on various issues. Talks were going smoothly when Packer demanded exclusive television rights in Australia when the existing agreement with the Australian Broadcasting Commission (ABC) expired early in 1979. The ICC refused point blank and the talks finished on a bitter note.

Outside the Lord's committee room, a frustrated Packer told reporters on 14 May 1977:

> I am only in the arena because of my disagreement with the ACB. Had I got those TV rights, I was prepared to withdraw from the scene and leave the running of cricket to

the Board. I will now take no steps to help anyone, every man for himself and the devil take the hindmost. I compromised so much that I felt strange in myself. I thought we were going to reach a period of breakthrough but the talks failed because of the stubbornness of the ICC. I have never wanted to control cricket, but I wanted and I would have expected to get exclusive rights when the current TV contracts ran out. I said I would go back under the control of the Australian Board, have shorter tours and withdraw from the scene completely if our network could have these rights and the players were not victimised.

According to McFarline, even a staunch Packer supporter like Rod Marsh was amazed by these remarks. As he wrote in *A Game Divided*, 'Marsh, like the other senior players, had been lauding Mr Packer as the saviour of cricket. Now it appeared Mr Packer's interest in the game was not what it was thought to be.'

Before the negotiations broke down, Packer had said, 'We'll do what we can to co-operate with the cricket authorities. And if they co-operate with us there's no reason Test cricket should be disrupted.'

When the ICC and England's Test and County Cricket Board tried to enforce a Test and first-class match selection ban on the defectors on July 27, Packer backed a successful High Court challenge against the 'restraints of trade'.

With the help of Cornell and Robertson, Packer set up an unthinkable assignment of organising World Series Cricket to be played on alternative cricket grounds in Australia within three months. What looked a pipe dream of Supertests between Australian, West Indians and World XIs became a reality. Former Test greats Richie Benaud, Ian Chappell, Garry Sobers, Fred Trueman, Bill Lawry, Keith Stackpole and John Gleeson, among others, were used as consultants, commentators and ambassadors for this innovation.

VFL Park in Melbourne was the first venue for a Supertest on 2 December 1977. In this inaugural match, West Indians defeated Australians in an exciting low-scoring match, Viv Richards top-scored with 79 and 56. The other Richards, Barry from South Africa, played a magnificent innings of 207 for the World XI in the Gloucester Park Supertest on 27 January 1978. A fortnight later, Greg Chappell stroked a gritty and unbeaten 246 at the VFL Park.

Despite these marvellous performances, spectator interest was below the high expectation and Packer's Consolidated Group lost about $6 million in the first year. As the crowd response was significantly higher for the official Test series between Australia and India, it was thought that Packer might retreat. Far from it! He went full steam ahead with help from a new chief executive, Andrew Caro, in March 1978. With new innovations, such as floodlight night cricket, white ball, colour clothing and catchy chants like 'C'mon Aussie C'mon, C'mon' (by the advertising firm Mojo), the crowds eventually took to Supertests in a big way.

A day–night match between Australians and West Indians on 28 November 1978 attracted over 50,000 in Sydney. But the quality of batsmanship suffered with the fast bowlers dominating the scene. To quote Haigh, 'By the end of 1978–79 summer, it was in the interest of both sides to resolve their differences. The failure of the Ashes series had severely depleted the finances of the ACB and its member associations.' The same feeling was shared by other countries. The authorities in England, West Indies and Pakistan were under public pressure to re-assimilate the WSC signatories.

Soon Packer got what he wanted. Not only did his Channel 9 usurp the ABC but his Consolidated Press's PBL Marketing arm was awarded promotional rights to the official matches.

Television commentator Mark Nicholas colourfully sums up World Series Cricket in *Cricinfo*:

WSC was Kerry Packer's astonishing 18-month raid on the game, from late summer 1977 to the spring of 1979, when most of the world's best players deserted the established corridors and signed to play for Packer in the closest thing cricket has ever seen to a rock 'n roll circus. WSC was a mixture of day time and night time, red balls and white balls, piped clothing, pink clothing, sky blue and canary yellow, bouncers, helmets, drop-in pitches, and two Richards from previously untouchable boundaries, Barry and Viv, batting together in the same team. It was played upcountry and in urban centres, in show grounds and in parks and even, occasionally, on cricket grounds.

After this 'astonishing 18-month raid' the game was back to normal as cricket in Australia was run by the Australian Cricket Board, later to be named Cricket Australia. Despite the traumas of a few years, which spoilt many friendships, it improved the finances of international cricketers and added pleasure to those who watched cricket live or on television.

Triple treats for WSC

BARRY RICHARDS SCORED A BRILLIANT 207 in 296 minutes for the WSC World XI against WSC Australia in the Supertest at Gloucester Park in Perth in January 1978. For the opening wicket he added 369 runs with Gordon Greenidge who stroked 140. Then Viv Richards thrashed the Australian attack to make 177. The two magnificent Richards firing together is remembered by everyone who saw it on the field or on TV. At stumps on the opening day, the World XI was 1 for 433.

Dennis Lillee captured 7 for 23 to rout a strong West Indies lineup for 89 in the fourth Supertest between WSC Australia and WSC West Indies XI in Sydney in January 1979. In a blitzkrieg not acknowledged in record books, he dismissed six of the seven quality batsmen. He was at his intimidating best. He later said that it was the best he had bowled in international cricket, surpassing his 8 for 29 for Australia against the Rest of the World in Perth in 1971–72.

Greg Chappell was scintillating in the West Indies in1979 when he smashed three centuries. In the Port–of–Spain Supertest in March, he came in to bat in a crisis, WSC Australia having lost two wickets for no runs and made 150 of the best and Australia won by 24 runs.

Quotes against WSC

ROBIN MARLAR, ENGLAND'S CRICKET WRITER: 'THE use of private promotional money to establish top–class cricket outside the international framework is undesirable.'

Ray Steele, Australian Cricket Board of Control treasurer: 'People think I'm crook on cricket circuses. I'm not. I think there's place for that kind of cricket—some place in Siberia.'

Eric Beecher, editor of *Cricketer* in January 1978: 'The cricket revolution, as the Packer people have been representing it, is in cricket terms hardly more than a big, expensive bore.'

Quotes for WSC

KERRY PACKER: 'IF YOU WANT TO look at circuses, you'd better look at Australia fielding its third XI.'

Tony Greig: 'We've been accused of betraying the game because we decided to play for the money we think we're worth.'

Viv Richards: 'I feel privileged to have been personally involved in something which shook the cobwebs out of our game, breathed new life into it and elevated the professional cricketer to a financial status he had never before enjoyed.'

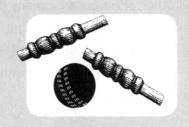

12

HOW THE D'OLIVEIRA AFFAIR DISMANTLED APARTHEID

If politics should not come in way of sports, how about sports coming in way of politics and triumphing? The D'Oliveira affair did just that. It has been cricket's greatest contribution to humanity. South Africa's hated apartheid (separate development policy for whites, blacks and coloureds) had been going on for centuries. Trade bans and other ploys used by many countries had little effect. Possibly, apartheid would have still been going on but for a chain of events that started in 1968 and ended with the sports isolation of South Africa for about two decades. In a large way, their isolation from international sports dismantled apartheid in a country that loves sports.

The Basil D'Oliveira story is inspirational. He was a promising non-white cricketer of Indian-Portuguese heritage from Cape Town who grew up in an impoverished area known as Signal Hill. He should have represented South Africa but for the colour of his skin. He was talented and popular but was debarred from representing his province or country because of being a 'Cape Coloured'. In non-white matches in Cape Town he had scored more than 50 centuries, including an aggressive innings of 225 in 70 minutes.

This is how the drama unfolded. It was the fifth and final Test of the Ashes Test at The Oval in London in August 1968; a must-win Test for England as Australia was leading 1–0. D'Oliviera was not in the original Eleven but Roger Prideaux withdrew because of pleurisy and in came 'Dolly' in his place.

Rather than give up, he continued performing in minor cricket with dazzling success on matting wickets and on poor pitches. Word about this young cricketer, whose talent was being ignored in the country of his birth, even reached England via prominent cricket writer John Arlott. D'Oliveira was offered £450 in 1960 to play for the Central Lancashire League Club in Middleton. For his airfare to England, £200 was needed and the sum was partially raised by fêtes, raffles and matches held in the region of his new home. In his first season for Middleton he outscored the great Garry Sobers. Soon he was to jump ladders of fame.

'Dolly', as he was popularly known, moved from poverty in Cape Town to relative prosperity in Worcestershire and eventually to Test fame. For

Worcestershire, 'Dolly' hit a century against the touring Australians in 1964 and the following season he hit five Championship hundreds, took 35 wickets with his medium–pace swing bowling and pouched some brilliant slip catches. In June 1966, he made his Test debut against the West Indies at Lord's. In the next Test at Trent Bridge he scored 76 and 54 followed by 88 in his third Test at Headingley. He was then 35 (or possibly 38 as his date of birth remains unclear) when most cricketers are considering retirement. His selection in the Test squad that season provoked a headline in England's *Daily Mirror*: 'HELLO DOLLY!'

Now to 1968 and how D'Oliveira changed the policy of racial segregation as never before. He was the catalyst behind the dismantling of apartheid in the country of his birth. Indirectly, so were the English selectors and by serendipity England's medium–pacer Tom Cartwright.

This is how the drama unfolded. It was the fifth and final Test of the Ashes Test at The Oval in London in August 1968; a must–win Test for England as Australia was leading 1–0. D'Oliviera was not in the original Eleven but Roger Prideaux withdrew because of pleurisy and in came 'Dolly' in his place.

England won that Test by 226 runs with only five minutes to spare and drew the series one–all. The heroes for England were Derek Underwood who captured 7 for 50 in the second innings and D'Oliveira who scored a lucky 158 runs in the first innings He was dropped four times and in the second innings had economical figures of one wicket for one run in 5 overs, four being maidens. It was an outstanding performance. On form he was a certainty for the tour to South Africa a few months later.

On the very night England had levelled the series with minutes to spare, the five men selection committee had a job on hand, to select a 16–man squad to South Africa. They faced a dilemma. D'Oliveira was a Cape Coloured and under South Africa's abhorrent apartheid laws he was considered a second–class citizen; not allowed to travel in the same train as the whites, to eat in the same restaurants as the whites or swim in the 'whites only' beaches or get their children educated in the whites' school. And certainly not play cricket with the whites. In the late 1960s, apartheid was at its worst, famous reform activist Nelson Mandela had by then started a 27–year jail term on Robben Island.

Many in England were not aware that South Africa's Prime Minister B.J. (John)

Vorster had told Viscount Cobham, a former MCC president, that D'Oliveira would be unacceptable. Ken Piesse wrote in *Cricket's Greatest Scandals* (2001) that the above 'message had been passed on to a select few at MCC. Inexplicably, the selectors hadn't been told and it created a furore in itself'.

When the message reached the selectors, D'Oliveira was dropped and cricket-lovers in England and elsewhere were shocked. Was it on cricketing grounds or was it a political issue?

A harassed selection chairman, Doug Insole, explained that D'Oliveira's bowling did not rate highly enough for him to be considered a genuine all-rounder. No one believed this explanation and there were howls of protest in England and overseas. Most were convinced that the selectors were swayed by political pressures and their judgement was affected. The media had a field day as politicians argued, administrators resigned and a strong protest group formed.

A week after the selection controversy, an injured medium-pacer Tom Cartwright withdrew from the selected squad and D'Oliveira took his place. A divine intervention, no less! D'Oliveira was in Plymouth having lunch with his wife and friends when he heard the news and wrote in his autobiography *The D'Oliveira Affair* (ghosted by Pat Murphy, 1969), 'It was the greatest moment I can remember.'

The South African Cricket Association immediately interjected and threatened to cancel the tour if D'Oliveira was in the squad. The consequences of the tour cancellation proved disastrous for South African cricket. If it was an earthquake, it would have been on a Richter scale of 8.5.

The D'Oliveira affair had a massive impact in turning international opinion against the oppressive apartheid regime in South Africa. It prompted changes in South African sport and eventually in society.

Going through the history of apartheid, André Odendaal wrote in his excellent book *Cricket in Isolation* (1977):

It was long before the D'Oliveira affair though that the first salvos were fired in the battle to ostracise the South African polecat... Not long after this, in 1961, South Africa lost its membership of the Imperial Cricket Conference, becoming the third white South African sports body to be excluded from international organisations.

South Africa had been ostracised in global sports beginning in the 1950s with table tennis. By 1964, anti-apartheid organisers had succeeded in getting the country barred from that year's Olympics, and in 1970 the International Olympic Committee expelled the country from the Olympic movement.

The country's absence from international sports rankled South Africans. South Africa had been selecting exclusively white cricket teams for Test matches since 1889. As the game blossomed in places like the Caribbean, India and Pakistan, South Africa found itself playing mostly white teams from England, Australia and New Zealand. Peter Oborne, wrote in *Basil D'Oliveira, Cricket and Conspiracy: The Untold Story* (2004) that the cricket authorities justified this by saying that cricket was a sport for whites, and that if blacks or coloureds did take it up, they 'played at an abysmally low level'. It was adding insult to injury.

The sad victims of the isolation of cricket in South Africa were their white cricketers, a majority of them would have loved to have coloureds and blacks in the national team provided they merited selection. And in their eyes Basil D'Oliveira certainly deserved selection. The South African cricket team that thrashed Australia 4-0 in 1970 was so strong they would have ruled international cricket for a decade and were described as 'Invincibles' in 1970s.

Just have a look at their 1970 team: Barry Richards, Graeme Pollock, Mike Procter, Peter Pollock, Trevor Goddard, Ali Bacher (captain), Eddie Barlow, Brian Irvine, Denis Lindsay… The first four can be classed legendary. At their best in 1970s, they missed Test cricket for the rest of their careers through no fault of theirs. By the time they were readmitted in Test fold in 1991–92, their magnificent Test careers had sadly gone with the wind of apartheid.

Their tours to England in 1970 and to Australia in 1971–72 were cancelled due to massive demonstrations by anti-apartheid protesters. These tours were replaced by Rest of the World teams, both including South African cricketers; Graeme and Peter Pollock, Barry Richards, Mike Procter and Eddie Barlow for the 1970 tour to England and Graeme and Peter Pollock and Hylton Ackerman for the 1971–72 Australian tour. Both the sides were captained by the legendary all-rounder Garry Sobers. The South African cricketers were welcomed effusively by the crowds in both countries.

I had the pleasure of interviewing Peter Pollock when he was in Sydney during the international series in January 1972. When I asked him whether he had any message for India, he replied solemnly and sincerely, 'I just hope one day things get sorted out and we tour India and India can visit us. It would be nice playing Tests in India, West Indies and Pakistan and being watched by so many cricket enthusiasts.' He had a wistful smile, dreaming of that day.

He also told me that a few months before this interview he and some other South African cricketers had staged a protest walk-off against the racial policy of their Government. Unfortunately, the protest had no significant effect.

The boycott of South Africa in cricket, as with other sports, remained till racial segregation was removed not only on the sporting arenas but also at other levels. It was a big victory for sports as it dismantled the abhorrent policy of apartheid.

Although Peter Pollock had retired from cricket and had become a lay preacher, his dream of his country playing internationally against all countries came true on 10 November 1991 when South Africa played a one-day international against India in Kolkata watched by about 90 000 cricket lovers. A historic match, it was the first-ever cricket encounter between South Africa and India.

It was 21 years and eight months after South Africa had played their last international, the Port Elizabeth Test against Australia, which they had won by 323 runs on 10 March 1970.

Their two decades of isolation in cricket had finally ended. In their World Cup debut, in the 1991–92 World Cup match in Sydney on 26 February 1992, the unified team defeated Australia by nine wickets. Two months later they played their first Test against the West Indies at Barbados, which the home team won by 52 runs on 18 April 1992.

I could imagine the smile of satisfaction on Peter Pollock's face when his son Shaun played 108 Tests from 1995 to 2008 for the unified South Africa. Shaun went on to become one of the best all-rounders with 3781 runs at 32.31 and 421 wickets at 23.11. He also captained his country with success and saw the development of fast bowler Makhaya Ntini, South Africa's first black African international cricketer.

Basil D'Oliveira must have died a happy man in 2011 when he saw revolutionary changes for the better, just because he was picked in the England team to tour South Africa in 1968. All he wanted was to play international cricket in the country of his birth. He did not realise this dream but achieved much more. From 2004 onwards, the Test series between South Africa and England is named The Basil D'Oliveira Trophy.

[13]
THE REBEL
TOURS TO SOUTH
AFRICA

T he previous chapter is like a novel with a compelling beginning and a happy ending. This chapter provides the middle that completes the story.

Decades of isolation from international cricket had robbed South Africa of its best years at the top. The political regime of their Prime Minister John Vorster had robbed the greats of the game in the 1970s—Barry Richards, Peter and Graeme Pollock, Mike Procter among others—of reaching their full potential. Officially, South African cricket (in fact all sports) was ostracised in 1970. This led to rebel tours to South Africa by teams from England, Australia, the West Indies and Sri Lanka in the 1980s.

As Chris Harte and Warwick Hadfield wrote in *Cricket Rebels* (1985):

In what has happened since [1970] lies the genesis of the 'rebel' tours of South Africa by an Australian side under the captaincy of Kim Hughes. His team is not the first. Since 1982, Englishmen, Sri Lankans and West Indians have made the tour. Like the South Africans, they do not like the term 'rebel' which they have attracted. But they are in rebellion against the policies of the Test match playing countries, England, Australia, New Zealand, West Indies, Pakistan, India and Sri Lanka which comprise the ruling body–the International Cricket Conference.

For receiving large sums of money, the so–called rebels had breached those policies for which they suffered the consequences. For their unofficial tours to South Africa, the English players were banned for three years, the Sri Lankans for 25 years and the West Indians for life. In the Caribbean, South Africa's policy of apartheid is considered a big evil.

For receiving large sums of money, the so–called rebels had breached those policies for which they suffered the consequences. For their unofficial tours to South Africa, the English players were banned for three years, the Sri Lankans for 25 years and the West Indians for life. In the Caribbean, South Africa's policy of apartheid is considered a big evil.

'In 1970, the world cricketing powers sent South Africa away with a list of things to put right to make cricket multi–racial,' continued Harte and Hadfield. 'To the consternation of many and the despair of few, South Africa had achieved most of the goals by mid-1970s. In 1977, the multi-racial South African Cricket Union was formed.'

South Africa's white cricketers had informed the government that they believed in the non-racial development of cricket. It climaxed in 1971 with the famous walk-off at the Newlands ground in Cape Town when leading players Eddie Barlow, Graeme Pollock, Peter Pollock and Mike Procter walked off from a high profile match, which was part of the Republic Festival celebration. The cricketing greats were in support of a move to include two coloured cricketers, Gesant Abed and Owen Williams, in the team to tour Australia in 1971-72. It was not granted and the tour was eventually cancelled.

However, wheels were moving forward, slowly but surely, towards the integration of blacks with whites in sporting arenas if not in social circles. In 1976, Richie Benaud, the legendary all-rounder and a balanced critic, managed an Australian XI captained by Greg Chappell to South Africa. Benaud was satisfied with the changes he had seen since he had toured South Africa with an official Australian side in 1963-64. He conceded that more had to be done but the changes were being made for the better. It was a step in the right direction.

But the Gleneagles Agreement drawn up between leaders of the Commonwealth in 1977 ended all hopes of South Africa being readmitted to the international sports arena. The refusal of the ICC in 1982 to allow the South Africans to present a report on what they had achieved since 1970 to make cricket multi-racial in the republic could be termed unwise. South African authorities may not have achieved enough towards multi-racial cricket, but they had every right to be heard and then be judged.

Dr Ali Bacher, the last captain of South Africa before the boycott in 1970, was feeling frustrated and by July 1982 lost all hopes of his country ever being readmitted into Test fold. That's when the idea of having rebel tours, with players offered good money, was hatched by him and Board members of the South African Cricket Union, Joe Pamensky and Geoff Dakin.

As reported in *Cricket Rebels*, Bacher said, 'It just hit me there and then to forget getting back into the world of cricket through the front door. We were on our own and we had to look after ourselves.'

Looking after ourselves meant offering Test players from around the world large sums of money to play unofficial international cricket matches. He continued, 'I am fighting for the survival of South African cricket, for the game that I love which has been the most important part of my life.'

This is going ahead of the story of intrigue and mystique; how Bacher went ahead with the signing of Australian Test players in Singapore's Paramount Hotel in 1982. The Australians under Kim Hughes played a series of five one–day internationals in India in September–October 1984 to celebrate the Golden Jubilee of the Ranji Trophy.

He soon started 'Operation Bacher', as secretive as James Bond assignments and just as daring. His bid for an Australian team commenced in March 1982 when he contacted Bruce Francis, a former Australian Test opener, in strict confidence. After retiring from cricket, Francis had remained close to the game, getting involved in the establishment of World Series Cricket in 1977 and subsequently he was a key factor in the rebel Australian tour to South Africa in 1984–85.

Francis was convinced that South Africa should be readmitted to cricket. 'He had a profound knowledge of South African history, its cricket, its politics and knew more about the Gleneagles Agreement than most politicians,' wrote Harte and Hadfield in *Cricket Rebels*. He was an academic and South African studies were part of his degree at the University of Sydney.

His interest in South Africa was enhanced when touring that country in 1973 with an invitation team organised by Derrick Robins. Francis passionately felt that contact and not isolation was the key to dismantle apartheid. He wrote a strong and lengthy letter to Bob Hawke, then the Prime Minister of Australia, on 6 August 1985, to allow exchange of official tours between Australia and South Africa. But it had little effect.

This is going ahead of the story of intrigue and mystique; how Bacher went ahead with the signing of Australian Test players in Singapore's Paramount Hotel in 1982. The Australians under Kim Hughes played a series of 5 one-day internationals in India in September–October 1984 to celebrate the Golden Jubilee of the Ranji Trophy. Australia won the series 3–0 but some cloak and dagger events were on the calendar. On their way home several of the Australian cricketers had their first significant contact with Ali Bacher and representatives of the South African Cricket Union.

Clandestine meetings with the Bacher group took place in Singapore, which led to another major crisis for the Australian cricket authorities. This is how Ken Piesse describes those meetings in Paramount Hotel, Singapore, in *Cricket's Greatest Scandals* (2001):

> Upstairs in the biggest room he could book, Bacher, the recruiting power behind the South African Cricket Union's rebel tours, was looking to consummate a two-year agreement for a long-awaited Australian visit to the Republic [of South Africa]. He'd gone close in 1983 before negotiations stalled. This time he had a A$3 million budget with large advances to the 14 or 15 players prepared to sign.

South African cricket bodies were getting frustrated as they were not allowed to speak at the International Cricket Conference. Also, three of their key administrators were refused visas to enter Australia.

When England, West Indies and Sri Lanka toured South Africa in early 1980s, Australia's cricket-loving Prime Minister, Bob Hawke, met leading Australian players at The Oval in London during the 1983 World Cup. He made it clear to them that until apartheid was abolished in South Africa there should not be any contact with the Republic. There was an indirect threat of government intervention should any cricketer turn renegade.

Australia's cricket-loving Prime Minister, Bob Hawke, met leading Australian players at The Oval in London during the 1983 World Cup. He made it clear to them that until apartheid was abolished in South Africa there should not be any contact with the Republic. There was an indirect threat of government intervention should any cricketer turn renegade.

Notwithstanding this ultimatum, some Australian cricketers were having a series of meetings with Bacher and showing enthusiasm for a tour to the Republic and handsome tax-free payments. Although the top-tiered 16 players were paid well (A$65 000) in Australia, the rest were still paid pittance.

Also, Bacher told the Australian players in Singapore that not only would they be well rewarded financially, they would be playing against the world's best cricketers at some of the best venues. And they would be opposing apartheid by direct contact rather than by ostracism.

The players flew back to Australia with an oath of secrecy. Nine of those present during the Singapore meeting, including Kim Hughes, were shortly named in Australia's first Test team against the West Indies at Perth.

But there was a sub-plot, the teary farewell to Test captaincy by Hughes. His Test career from 1977 to 1984 coincided with major confrontations; the World Series Cricket (WSC) revolution, which he opposed strongly; rebel tours to South Africa–a big no–no in 1980s–and the pace–like–fire of the West Indies fast bowlers Michael Holding, Malcolm Marshall and Joel Garner, which tarnished many batsmen's reputations. He also unwisely decided to take WSC protagonists Ian Chappell and Rod Marsh head–on.

It seemed everything conspired to let the ambitious baby–faced tousle–haired Kim down. His Waterloo came during the 1984–85 series against Clive Lloyd's all-conquering West Indies team. If only his performances as a batsman and captain matched his pre–Test bravado, he could have surfaced from the crises. However, the pressures and unrelenting criticism affected his batting and thinking and his slide was rapid.

An emotional person, Hughes often appeared to be his own worst enemy. His complaints against Ian Chappell and Marsh were chilli–hot and the Australian media had a ball using them in large fonts. But he failed to back up his brave words with runs or wins after 1982.

He had thus far won only four of the 26 Tests captained. He had psyched himself to produce his best against the 'invincible' West Indies in 1984–85 but he had under him a divided Australian team. Despite his brave words, Australia lost the first Test in Perth by an innings after being skittled out for only 76 in the first innings. He made 4 and 37.

The second Test in Brisbane was just as disastrous. Australia lost by eight wickets on the fourth day, Hughes making 34 and 4. He immediately resigned as captain. In an emotional post–match press conference he said in a prepared statement, trying to hold back tears: 'The constant criticism, speculation and innuendo by former players and a section of the media over the past four or five years have finally taken their toll.' He was so choked with emotion that team manager Bob Merriman had to finish reading the statement.

As Australia had lost both the Tests convincingly, it appeared to some that Hughes was leaving a sinking ship. 'Not so,' wrote Peter McFarline in *Wisden Cricket Monthly* of January 1985. According to McFarline, Hughes had been placed in an untenable position by some leading officials on the Board. He was told firmly that he was unlikely to hold the leadership for the rest of the series because his captaincy was not worthy of international standard.

Hughes also felt that he was losing the support of the team under him. When he told the Australian Cricket Board about his intention to resign, no one tried to talk him out of this decision. He also thought that without the burden of captaincy he might regain his batting form in the remaining Tests in the series. Far from it! Under new skipper Allan Border, he scored a first ball duck and two in Adelaide and a pair in Melbourne, which turned out to be his final Test.

For much of the 1985 summer there were hints that another major revolution was brewing in Australian cricket. Just after the team to England had been selected in early March, the rumours were confirmed when ABC's Jim Maxwell broke the story on national radio. Within 36 hours it was front page news. 'It was like a bomb going off,' wrote Ken Piesse:

> It was World Series Cricket again except this time Packer was in bed with ACB (Australian Cricket Board). Believing they'd been undermined by cricketers too mercenary for their own good, the ACB threatened 10-year bans on prospective rebels who refused to sign statutory declarations saying they wouldn't tour South Africa.

The ACB also denounced the South Africa Cricket Union (SACA), declaring it as guilty as the players who would sign with them. The politicians joined in, denouncing the SACA and the players who would join in the rebel tours. Prime Minister Bob Hawke accused the rebels of prejudicing the future of Australian cricket, suggesting that other countries may refuse to play Australia at international level. However, at government level there was no inquisition on trade with South Africa, Ken Piesse added cynically.

Meanwhile seven of the 17 selected to tour England for the Ashes had signed with Bacher's breakaways. But in a dramatic turnaround, four of them— Graeme Wood, Murray Bennett, Wayne Phillips and Dirk Wellham—signed

ACB's declaration and withdrew from the tour to South Africa. Wellham was immediately rewarded with a A$45 000 three-year scholarship from Packer's PBL Marketing. However, Carl Rackemann, Terry Alderman and Rod McCurdy remained with Bacher.

The latest developments concerning the rebel tours were given more prominence in the media than the results of the disappointing Ashes tour. After weeks of legal battles, there was an out of court truce. The South African Cricket Union agreed to pay A$120 000 of ACB's legal cost and promised that there would be no further 'raids'.

Bans were still imposed on those who joined the rebel tours; three years from Test cricket and two years from the Sheffield Shield. Of the 16 rebels to South Africa in 1985–86, only three—Rackemann, Alderman and Trevor Hohns—later represented Australia in Test cricket.

According to famous cricket writer Steven Lynch in *Cricinfo*:

Bacher saw the post–[Nelson] Mandela writing on the wall, put away the cheque-book, and reinvented himself as South Africa's cricket supremo when the previously separate black and white associations combined to set up the United Cricket Board. Bacher's reward came when his country marched back onto the international scene at the 1992 World Cup.

MEANWHILE, WHAT ABOUT KIM HUGHES, ONE of the most talented but less liked Test batsman? With his Test career in tatters (after scoring 0, 2, 0 and 0 in his final four Test innings) he led the Rebel Australians to South Africa in 1985–86 and 1986–87 without recapturing his glory of yesteryears. The third unofficial 'test' against South Africa at Johannesburg in 1985–86 was traumatic for him. He was dismissed first ball in both innings—a King Pair. But wait, there is more! Going in as Rodney Hogg's runner, he was run out first ball. So he went to the middle three times with a bat in hand in one match and returned all three times first ball. A new word was coined by me in my book *Out for a Duck* (1993), an Emperor Pair!

[14]
POPULAR BEDI'S
DESPERATE
'DECLARATION'

B ishan Bedi, India's left–arm spinner and later captain, was a popular character. Feared by opposing batsmen, the turbaned and bearded Sikh was loved by spectators around the world, especially in Australia. I remember watching him on the field in the Sydney international, representing the World XI under Garry Sobers in 1971–72. He had only to touch the ball and the crowd on the Hill would go crazy chanting 'Baidi, Baidi'. According to Australia's well–loved cricket writer Ray Robinson, 'Bedi was as popular in Australia as were England's Denis Compton and "Patsy" Hendren.'

Bedi's popularity was such that he was interviewed not only in sports magazines but also in women's magazines in Australia, till then the prerogative of Elizabeth Taylor, Jackie Onassis and Sonia McMahon. When a female interviewer asked him as to why the Australian crowds get so delirious just to see him play a ball, he smiled and said, 'I think the crowd likes something different and I do look different in my many coloured parka [turban]. Also they know I like your beer!'

Endearingly known as 'Bish' or 'Bishie' in Australia, he performed well in the unofficial tests for the World XI. He was at his best in the Test series for India against Australia in 1977–78, capturing 31 wickets at 23.87 in five Tests. He led the team with flair, although India lost the seesawing Test series 2–3. It remains one of the most exciting series ever, and is historic too as it coincided with the inaugural World Series Cricket played at the same time in Australia.

But Bedi is remembered more for the 1976 tour to the Caribbean where he received both bouquets and brickbats. This was one of the strongest West Indian sides with world-class batsmen Vivian Richards and Alvin Kallicharran, skipper Clive Lloyd, openers Roy Fredericks and Lawrence Rowe, all–rounder Bernard Julien and express fast bowlers Michael 'whispering death' Holding, Andy Roberts and Wayne 'Black Diamond' Daniel as also accurate fast–medium Vanburn Holder.

After losing the first Test at Barbados by an innings, India showed marked improvement in the drawn second Test at Port–of–Spain, thanks to master batsman Sunil Gavaskar (156) and Brijesh Patel (115 not out) adding 204 runs for the fifth wicket and Bedi taking 5 for 82 and 3 for 44. Due to incessant rains in Guyana, the third Test was moved to Port–of–Spain. And what a match it was— with an incredible finish!

Set 403 runs to win in 10 hours, India reached the target with six wickets and 30 minutes remaining. The total of 4 for 406 was then the highest in the fourth innings to win a Test. Prior to this fascinating victory there was only one instance of a side scoring over 400 runs in the fourth innings to win a Test; Australia under Don Bradman had amassed 3 for 404 to win the 1948 Leeds Test against England.

India's victory was mainly due to Gavaskar and Gundappa Viswanath (later to become his brother–in–law) hitting centuries and Mohinder Amarnath, the son of Lala Amarnath (see chapter 7) playing the anchor role with 85. It was India's finest hour and Bedi was the flavour of the month for instructing his batsmen to go for runs rather than play for a boring draw.

Endearingly known as 'Bish' or 'Bishie' in Australia, he performed well in the unofficial tests for the World XI. He was at his best in the Test series for India against Australia in 1977–78, capturing 31 wickets at 23.87 in five Tests.

But the fourth and final Test, a fortnight later in Kingston, Jamaica, proved disastrous for both India and Bedi. Call it from sublime to shattered, from ecstasy to agony—the recently relaid pitch was heaven for West Indies fast bowlers and hell for the Indian batsmen. The home side won the toss and decided to bowl. India started well and at one stage were one down for 205 with good contributions from Gavaskar, Anshuman Gaekwad and Mohinder Amarnath. But the pitch had uneven bounce, which differed vastly at the two ends. There was a surfeit of short–pitched deliveries, especially from Holding, among the fastest and most accurate fast bowlers ever. Three batsmen were seriously injured during this innings, Viswanath was dismissed by a ball that fractured and dislocated his right middle finger, Gaekwad was struck on the left ear and was hospitalised for two days and Patel had three stitches inserted in his mouth.

Bedi declared the innings closed at 6 for 306 as a protest against the intimidatory bowling. He also did not wish the tailenders (B.S. Chandrasekhar and himself) to get injured as they were needed as spin bowlers when the West Indians batted. Chandrasekhar took five wickets and the Windies led by 85 runs. Then the incredible drama began in India's second innings. Only six batted as the other five batsmen were injured. India made a low score of 97 and lost the Test by 10 wickets.

There was confusion as to whether India had declared at 5 for 97 or they were all out for 97 with five absent. Bedi stated that apart from the serious injuries to Viswanath, Gaekwad and Patel, neither Chandrasekhar nor he was fit to bat because of hand injuries sustained while fielding. Many felt that he was protecting the two top-line spinners from further injuries off the bowling of Holding et al. All seventeen members of the touring party fielded at some stage during the angry match, probably a Test first.

This debatable episode is explained in Suresh Menon's biography on *Bedi: Bishan – Portrait of a Cricketer* (2011). While too much is written on Bedi for this fluctuating series, spare a thought for the Windies skipper Lloyd. According to Menon, the knives were out for him. After leading the West Indies to a splendid win in the inaugural World Cup in 1975, he had lost the overseas Test series to Australia 1–5. They were not just defeated but routed by Australian pace bowlers Jeff Thomson, Dennis Lillee, Gary Gilmour and Max Walker. 'Another loss [to India] might have brought Lloyd's career as captain to an end,' wrote Menon. 'The West Indies needed to overhaul their thinking. Spin would not work.'

The West Indies spinners had claimed only five wickets among them in the Port–of–Spain Test as India raced to 4 for 406 to win the Test. The home team decided that the only way they could win was to pack the team with quickies, always their strength. 'When nothing works, try intimidation' has been their motto over the years. So the Windies went full steam ahead with fiery pace on a bouncy pitch with Holding bowling round the wicket at the batsmen. And one should remember that in those days there were no proper helmets and no protective pads.

As stated above, India started well but then the injury list grew as the match progressed. India lost the Test by ten wickets after losing only twelve wickets in two innings. Weird stuff! The Indians complained to the umpires but to no avail. At the press conference after the match, team manager Polly Umrigar said, 'Holding bowled three to four bouncers per over. The intimidation was persistent and his intention was clear when he went round the wicket to aim at the batsmen. There were enough grounds for the umpires to intervene under Law 46.'

Bedi added, 'I spoke to the umpire [Ralph] Gosein at lunch after Gaekwad and Viswanath were injured, but he only laughed.'

In his autobiography, *Living for Cricket* (1980), Lloyd wrote, 'I must say I felt a little sorry for them at the time, but there was certainly no deliberate policy on our part to indulge in unfair tactics.' He found an escape clause though when defending himself, his pace battery and the umpires by writing, 'In the pitch on the northern end there was a particular spot from which the ball would either fly dangerously or shoot. All the batsmen hit suffered their injuries at that end.'

Wisden 1977 commented about the short-pitched bowling that 'there was a surfeit of it—overdone in fact to the extent where the umpires should have intervened'. Dicky Rutnagar added, 'As at the end of the tour, the Indian team trudged along the tarmac towards their home-bound aeroplane at Kingston's Norman Manly Airport, they resembled Napoleon's troops on the retreat from Moscow. They were battle weary and a lot of them were enveloped in plasters and bandages.'

Here is an abstract from what Bedi had written to me about 'the ugly Jamaica Test' in a 6-page personal letter in June 1976:

Trinidad where India won the Test chasing 406 for a fabulous win was simply out of the world. After this win, we were looking forward to a good contest in the final six-day Test in Kingston, Jamaica, but what a fiasco it turned out to be. With plenty of bounce, I was apprehensive about our batting. So when Clive [Lloyd] won the toss and gave us the first strike, I wasn't terribly happy. I was almost sure the Test wouldn't last six days.

But against hostile pace from Holding, Daniel, Holder and Julien our three batters— Sunil Gavaskar, Anshuman Gaekwad and Mohinder Amarnath set the tempo. Sunil got ruffled getting five bumpers in an over from Holding and then getting out to the same bowler. Sunil, who had bruises to show, protested showing gestures of displeasure but the umpires took no notice. With India 205 for one, Clive instructed Holding to bowl round the wicket. It was a simple case of 'if you can't get them out, hit them out'. There were bumpers galore, three to four per over.

At lunch on the second day I asked the umpire to define 'intimidation' but they had no answer. I could never forgive them for not doing their job honestly. However by that time Clive was laughing 'cos [because] three of our main-line batters were out of the game; Gaekwad could have been killed, he was blue all over after being hit on the head.

I am sure Douglas Jardine must have turned in his grave, it was a display of Bodyline and the hostile Jamaican crowd loved it. The two gentlemen in white coats were too timid to put things right and my main complaint is against them. Holding carried out his captain's instructions remarkably well, full marks to him ... Two of the West Indies players confessed to me that they were nervous standing in slips lest anyone would be killed ... There should be legislation to curb intimidation. Cricket is too good a game to be associated with death.

As if this wasn't enough, myself and Chandrasekhar had fractured fingers while fielding, so it really became XI a side against VI a side. It was a shame to call it a Test match. Let me assure you that there was no ridge on the wicket. It was a lovely strip, fast and true, and had some turn for our spinners too.

I disagree with my friend Bishan on one issue. Lloyd's tactic in this Test cannot be called Bodyline because there was no packed leg-side field.

Reviewing Menon's *Bishan – Portrait of a Cricketer*, *Wisden* 2012 wrote:

The Bishan Bedi who emerges from these pages is capricious, cantankerous and feisty but undeniably A Good Thing ... Bedi's stand against intimidatory bowling of the West Indies looks far more courageous now than it did at that time. In a large way, this brave stand by Bedi led to the restrictions of bumpers per over which is good for the game.

Thus some good came out of the 1976 Jamaican speed–blitz after all.

BISHAN BEDI IS A COMPLEX CHARACTER—LIKEABLE, obstinate and funny. He once invited me to bowl against Indian batsmen at the SCG nets before their match against New South Wales in November 1977, a highlight of my low–key cricket career!

In the course of the match against New South Wales, Bedi returned to the pavilion. When I asked him why, he replied, 'I think I've swallowed a fly!'

Bedi has a lively sense of humour. Mushtaq Ali, the attacking Indian batsman (the Errol Flynn of Indian cricket, according to Keith Miller), had toured England in 1936, hitting a spectacular century in the Manchester Test. When he revisited England 60 years later he was shocked to see the changes. He told Bedi, 'Englishmen are not wearing hats these days.' Wisecracked Bedi: 'That's nothing, Mushtaq bhai. These days during summer on the beaches, women don't wear their bikini tops either!'

[15]
HOLDING AND
CROFT LOSE IT IN
NEW ZEALAND

The West Indies tour of New Zealand in 1980 is remembered as one of the most acrimonious Test series. It was New Zealand's first Test series victory at home, starting with a thrilling one-wicket win in the first Test in Dunedin followed by drawn Tests in Christchurch and Auckland. New Zealand led the mighty Windies on first innings in all three Tests. But the West Indians lost more than the Test series, they—especially their fast bowlers Michael Holding and Colin Croft—lost their cool. They also lost their reputation as a sporting team.

Prior to the tour the West Indians, led by Clive Lloyd, had annihilated Australia 2–0 in a 3–Test series, winning by ten wickets in Melbourne and by 408 runs in Adelaide.

The New Zealand tour started a few days after the final Test in Adelaide and the visitors looked jaded. Perhaps they took New Zealand too lightly. They were also without their ace batsman Viv Richards who was injured. Many umpiring decisions went against them but the way they reacted was shocking.

Both tour manager Willie Rodriguez and captain Lloyd said that there should be neutral umpires. Fair enough. But Rodriguez went overboard when stating that the West Indians had to get a batsman out nine times before getting a positive decision and claimed the West Indians were 'set up'.

Their confidence was low as they had lost the one–day international to New Zealand at Christchurch by one wicket as they struggled to get accustomed to the New Zealand conditions, vastly different from Australia's. Then started the controversial first Test in Dunedin, which they also lost by one wicket.

Winning the toss, Lloyd decided to bat on a lively pitch and the Windies were bowled out for 140, Richard Hadlee capturing 5 for 34. The Kiwis took a lead of 109 runs. The tourists could make only 212 in the second innings. Hadlee was again unplayable with 6 for 68, only opener Desmond Hayne stood firm with a gutsy 105 and set the home team an easy win target of 104. Hadlee's eleven wickets in the match included a Test record of seven lbw decisions.

Twenty minutes before lunch on the final day, 13 February, John Parker was given not out when Holding appealed for a catch by wicketkeeper Deryck Murray. Holding was so outraged he kept running down the pitch in his follow–through and demolished stumps at the batsman's end with a full swing of his right foot. Imagine the headlines in the daily press today at such boorish behaviour. Or how

Top left: Members of the First Australian XI who visited England in 1878 (image courtesy Cricket NSW).

Top right: English wicket-keeper Ted Pooley, who ended up in jail in New Zealand in 1876 for gambling on cricket results (image courtesy Ronald Cardwell Collection).

Above: Aussie legends of 1930s (left to right) Bert Oldfield, Bill Ponsford, Bill O'Reilly, Sir Donald Bradman, Stan McCabe (image courtesy Cricket NSW).

Left: Harold Larwood bowling his thunderbolt to Sir Donald Bradman (image courtesy Cricket NSW).

Far left top: West Indian bowling star Michael Holding was nicknamed 'Whispering Death' by international umpires.

Far left bottom: England fast bowler John Snow is grabbed by SCG patron Trevor Guy in 1971. The incident was a climax to some fiery bowling from Snow and led to a walk off by the English team.

Right: Sir Don Bradman's brilliance with the bat became the focal point of Douglas Jardine's 'Bodyline' bowling attack in the 1932-33 Ashes series.

Below right: South African-born Basil D'Oliveira's late selection for England for the tour of his former homeland in 1968 precipitated South Africa's exclusion from international competition.

Above left: Aron 'Ali' Bacher, South African captain against Australia in 1969-70, was selected to lead tours of England (1970) and Australia (1970-71), both of which were aborted due to his country's apartheid stance.

Above right: Bill O'Reilly, Bradman's teammate and, later, his sternest critic.

Below: Cricket umpire Tony Crafter separates Australian fast bowler Dennis Lillee, left, and Pakistani batsman Javed Miandad during an angry altercation in the 1981 Perth Test (AP via AAP).

Above: Australian television tycoon Kerry Packer, right, with former England cricket captain Tony Greig after a press conference at the Dorchester Hotel (PA via AAP).

Right: Peter Roebuck attired in his distinguishing straw hat at the SCG Press Box in 2001.

Above: Tony Greig presenting the Man of the Match award to Chris Broad.

Left: Former Australian off-spinner Ashley Mallet at the SCG, recalling the flaming Mumbai Test.

Below: Dirk Wellham all set to sign up with the Rebels.

Far right top: 'Two little Masters' — Sunil Gavaskar and Sir Donald Bradman.

Far right bottom: Michael Atherton watching the Sydney Test in 2003.

Left: Legendary Indian bowler Bishan Bedi. The left-arm spinner was a member of the famous 'Indian Spin Quartet'.

Below: Hansie Cronje raises his hand to take the oath in Cape Town 15 June 2000, prior to testifying before the King Commission of Inquiry into allegations of cricket match-fixing (AFP/AAP).

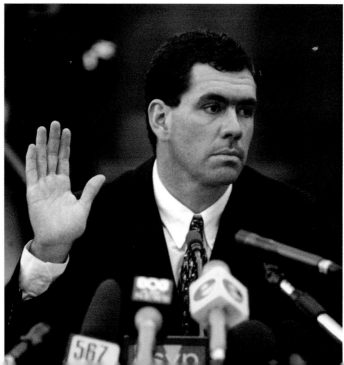

Holding himself, now an esteemed cricket commentator, would have castigated a bowler for similar behaviour.

Recalling Holding's stump-kicking incident, Goodall said, 'I ran from square-leg to Clive Lloyd and told him, "Excuse me skipper, would you like to have a quiet word with your players?" But there was no response from him. A slip fielder told me, "You're all cheats".'

By lunchtime the home team was struggling at 2 for 33 and soon after it was 7 for 54, they were still 50 runs short. It seemed that the Windies had won the match but Hadlee, Lance Cairns and Gary Troup resisted. It was 8 for 96 a little after tea when Holding 'bowled' Cairns. The ball hit the off stump without dislodging a bail. Naturally, Holding had that 'am-I-jinxed-or-what' sort of expression. He however dismissed Cairns a little later but New Zealand won the Test by one wicket off a leg bye!

The New Zealand tour started a few days after the final Test in Adelaide and the visitors looked jaded. Perhaps they took New Zealand too lightly. They were also without their ace batsman Viv Richards who was injured. Many umpiring decisions went against them but the way they reacted was shocking.

The second Test in Christchurch a week later was drawn and is remembered for another temper tantrum, this time by West Indian fast bowler Colin Croft. After being no-balled eleven times, Croft angrily flicked off the bails as he walked back in defiance. A little later he ran in to bowl close to the umpire, Goodall, and in the process shouldered the umpire heavily.

New Zealand's respected correspondent R.T. Brittenden wrote in *Wisden* 1981, 'It was the height of discourtesy when Goodall, wishing to speak to Lloyd about Croft's behaviour, had to walk all the way to the West Indian captain, standing deep in the slip. Lloyd took not a step to meet him.'

In this Test, Richard Hadlee hit his maiden Test century, which was a significant milestone. But he had a hollow feeling about it as the opponents did not bowl at their best. The West Indians packing their bags and threatening strike action was also distasteful to him.

After tea on the third day during the Christchurch Test, the West Indians refused to take the field for twelve minutes, saying that they would not continue unless umpire Goodall was removed. They were finally persuaded to continue. If Darrell Hair was the umpire, he would have had no hesitation in considering this absence as a forfeit and announced New Zealand as the winner. Refer to chapter 25, regarding the 2006 Test between England and Pakistan at The Oval.

That evening in Christchurch, there was a distinct possibility that the tour would be aborted. After prolonged negotiations between the West Indies tour management and the New Zealand Board of Control, it was agreed that the Test and the rest of the tour would continue. The NZ Board made it clear that Croft, after his 'attack' on Goodall, should not be included in the next Test in Auckland. However, he did play.

I recently interviewed New Zealand opening batsman Bruce Edgar who had played in all three Tests in this controversial series, scoring 65 in Dunedin and 127 in Auckland. This is what he said:

I think if this happened today, Croft would have been either stood down for few games or banned for some considerable time—even life—for deliberately 'assaulting' an umpire. Sure, the West Indies were frustrated after having beaten Australia on the way to New Zealand but became very petulant when things didn't go their way.

You may recall that Michael Holding also kicked two stumps out of the ground in the first Test in Dunedin, which NZ won. Prior to this Test they had also lost the ODI in Christchurch and then lost a provincial match against Wellington.

Now to the staying in the dressing room incident in Christchurch: Should they have been timed out? I'm sure if Darrell Hair had been umpiring in those days or the NZ umpires had more experience (at the time) to act, the West Indians would have been forced to forfeit the match. I also suspect the NZ officials didn't want to offend them, even though the West Indians had technically breached the rules.

And then to see that this tour did not even get a mention in the 'Fire in Babylon' documentary suggests that it was a series that 'never happened' or otherwise the West Indies invincibility story would have been diluted.

UNDERARM NOT
UNDERHAND

T he underarm incident on the Melbourne Cricket Ground on 1 February 1981 created as many international waves as the Bodyline series of 1932–33 and the rebel tours to South Africa in the 1980s, with politicians of two countries joining the journalists and former Test cricketers making strong comments.

Talk of *that* one-day international (ODI) between Australia and New Zealand on the MCG of 1981 and you remember Trevor Chappell, the reluctant executioner; Greg Chappell, the executive and Brian McKechnie, the disgruntled victim. But the man who was on the field all 100 overs, fielding and batting, is forgotten. He is the New Zealand left-hand opening batsman Bruce Edgar, now settled in Sydney, Australia.

I had the opportunity to discuss this event with him. 'I am amused when people ask me whether I played in that match,' he recalls. 'No one seems to remember that I had carried the bat scoring 102 not out and was at the bowler's end when the idea of bowling the underarm was conceived, discussed and executed.'

Let's revisit the thriller with a twist in the tail. It was the third final in a series of four. New Zealand had won the first in Sydney by 78 runs but lost the second in Melbourne by seven wickets. Thus the series was locked one-all with two matches to go.

Now to the third final and perhaps the most talked about ODI. The spectators had no inkling of what was to transpire till the last ball was bowled, rather underarmed! The first controversy of the match was when Greg Chappell was given not out when, according to Edgar, he was brilliantly caught by a diving Martin Snedden off Lance Cairns.

Greg Chappell, on 52 then went on to make 90. The visitors were already feeling peeved with him. Eventually, he was caught by Edgar and the innings ended. 'I caught him low down in the outfield and we were left to score 236 runs to win,' Edgar remembers. 'In fact, Snedden's catch (disallowed by the umpires) was more convincing than mine.'

Greg Chappell's version is given elsewhere in the chapter.

The Kiwis were on 6 for 221, needing fifteen runs, when the final over from Trevor Chappell began. Richard Hadlee straight drove the first ball for a four but was lbw off the second. Wicketkeeper, and now TV commentator, Ian Smith took two runs each off the next two deliveries and was bowled by the fifth. Score now

8 for 229. And in came Brian McKechnie, a rugby international, needing to hit a six off the last ball to tie the match.

'Take us through, Bruce, the last ball when you were at Trevor Chappell's end, with a century under your belt,' I asked:

There were discussions galore. Greg talking to Trevor and to the umpires Peter Cronin and Don Weser, the umpires informing Brian [McKechnie] and me about the underarm delivery, Rod Marsh imploring Greg not to go ahead with this strategy which will have damaging complications... Anyway, Trevor did as instructed. When the infamous underarm was bowled, Brian blocked the ball and tossed his bat to the ground in disgust. I also gave Trevor a two-fingered salute and uttered a couple of expletives but to no avail.

The New Zealand captain Geoff Howard, dressed casually in socks, rushed onto the field to protest. He had mistakenly believed underarm bowling to be illegal. (It was made illegal in Australia after this match.) The rest is history. The fallout was widespread. For this unwise ploy Greg was chastised by the Australian Cricket Board, Sir Donald Bradman, Australian Prime Minister Malcolm Fraser and New Zealand Prime Minister Robert Muldoon who called the underarm delivery 'an act of cowardice appropriate to a team playing in yellow'.

The rest is history. The fallout was widespread. For this unwise ploy Greg was chastised by the Australian Cricket Board, Sir Donald Bradman, Australian Prime Minister Malcolm Fraser and New Zealand Prime Minister Robert Muldoon who called the underarm delivery 'an act of cowardice appropriate to a team playing in yellow'.

Eldest brother Ian Chappell condemned this action by writing, 'Fair dinkum, Greg, how much pride do you sacrifice to win $35 000? Because, brother, you sacrificed a lot in front of a huge TV audience and 52 825 people.' When I interviewed Greg in 2010 for *Inside Cricket* magazine, he told me that he 'absolutely regretted the decision which was made in the heat of the moment'.

McKechnie recently said, 'Trevor didn't say sorry at the end of the match or the next day. We are on talking terms now and I have no ill feelings.'

Here is Greg Chappell's version of this highly controversial incident. He writes in his autobiography *Fierce Focus* (2011), 'By 1 February [1981], I wasn't fil enough to captain a rowboat, let alone the Australian cricket team.' He was exhausted from non-stop cricket and dejected after Australia lost the first ODI final in Sydney but bounced back to beat the Kiwis in Melbourne, not Greg's favourite ground. He confided, 'I was sick of the MCG, sick of the constant travelling and being away from home, and probably for the first time, sick of cricket.'

The bitterly controversial ODI in Melbourne started the day after the second ODI. When in his fifties, Greg went down the wicket to hit fast-medium bowler Lance Cairns, lifting it over midwicket. In the deep, Martin Snedden made a desperate lunge for the dropping ball. As Greg was running he could not see whether he was caught cleanly or not and so left it to the umpire. Greg noted, 'The umpires, Don Wesser and Peter Cronin, also could not see if Snedden had caught it ... The New Zealanders were frustrated, which I could understand.'

Greg was disappointed with the Australian fielding and felt that they were just going through the motions. He admitted, 'We could not afford to! If we lost, we'd need to take the series to the fifth match... The need to avoid a fifth match obsessed me.'

When he gave the last over to brother Trevor, Richie Benaud remarked that Greg had got his sums wrong. Greg disagrees with this comment stating that Trevor was a good choice to bowl on the sludgy pitch with his clever change of pace.

On the final underarm delivery, Greg wrote:

Commentators, including my brother Ian and Richie Benaud, accused me of doing something 'gutless', driven by fear, but that was not it at all. I was fed up with this place [MCG] and this game, I was fed up with my team's fielding, I was fed up with a thousand little things that all came to a head in that moment.

He was given cold treatment in the dressing room and criticised everywhere he went—by the journalists, commentators, administrators and politicians from both the countries. He admits that the decision to instruct Trevor to bowl underarm was although within the then laws of cricket was not within the spirit of the game. 'The decision was made whilst I was under pressure and in the heat of the moment,' he said. 'I regret the decision. It is something I would not do again. I'll never try to justify what I did. Asking Trevor to bowl underarm was a sign of my very poor mental state. I just wasn't myself.'

GREG CHAPPELL, AN ELEGANT AND MAJESTIC batsman, was the first cricketer to score a century in his first and final Test innings. He was also the first Australian to amass 7000 runs in Tests. His teammate Doug Walters wrote in the 'Foreword' of my book *Six Appeal* (1996), that it is possible to hit an underarm grubber for a six:

I came up with a solution as to how Brian McKechnie could have scored a six off that underarm grubber delivery. Allan Border bet me it was impossible to hit a rolling ball for a six. To prove my point I took him to the centre of the SCG No. 2 and asked him to bowl me a ball along the ground. I stepped down the pitch a few paces so that I could not be given out LBW and flicked the ball up with my foot. My bat connected with it at the correct time and it went flying over the fence. Border shook his head in disbelief. But I am still waiting for him to pay up!

Bruce Edgar, now my neighbour in Sydney, is a fitness fanatic, cycling hundreds of kilometres a day on occasions. His highest Test score of 161 was scored against Australia in the 1981 Auckland Test. It contributed richly to New Zealand's surprise victory over Australia. His 102 not out in the 1981 controversial MCG match is his only century in ODIs. The number 102 is so close to his heart that it forms part of his e-mail address. Also he is nicknamed Underarm Bruce and Rexona in his cycling group.

According to Greg Chappell, Edgar and John Wright were up with the best opening pairs in world cricket in early 1980s.

[17]
LILLEE, LILLEE,
LILLEE; OI, OI,
OUCH

I n my 60 years of cricket watching, I have seen and admired many fast bowlers but Dennis Lillee remains my favourite. Ray Lindwall, Fred Trueman, Frank Tyson, Wes Hall, Roy Gilchrist, Jeff Thomson, Andy Roberts, Malcolm Marshall were perhaps faster. But none, except Michael Holding, was as graceful, well-balanced, articulately accurate and venomously deadly as Lillee. From his international debut against Garry Sobers-led World XI in Perth in 1971, to his farewell Test in Sydney against Pakistan in Sydney in 1984, he has remained my *numéro uno* as a fast bowler.

The names Lillee and Thomson are so well linked that they were at one stage known as 'Lilian-Thomson' and there was that frightening quote: 'If Thommo doesn't get you, Lillee must.' Both were behind many Test victories for Australia with their menacing pace and hostile bouncers. To use a cricketing cliché, Lillee's bowling action was poetry in motion. He captured batsmen's scalps with his flowing hair doing a rhythmic tango with his bushy moustache. 'Quick to boil, he was quick to smile,' to quote Christopher Martin-Jenkins in *World Cricketers – a Biographical Dictionary* (1996). He was also a showman who converted non cricket-lovers to cricket addicts. I can still hear the chants of 'Lillee, Lillee, Lillee, oi, oi, oi' from the crowd. He had that certain presence ... menacing presence.

Lillee is featured in this book not so much for his elegantly fatal speed but for his maverick nature, defying authority too often and being involved in numerous controversies. Three of them are featured in this chapter.

THE ALUMINIUM BAT

One of his finest seasons was 1979–80 against England in Australia when he captured 23 wickets at 16.86 in three Tests but he smudged his image with a public display of arrogance in the first Test in Perth in December 1979. He came in to bat with an aluminium bat. After he scored three runs off four balls from Ian Botham, England's captain Mike Brearley objected to its use, saying the ball was getting unfairly battered.

When the umpires asked him to replace the aluminium bat to a normal wooden one, he argued with them. The match was held up for ten minutes and resumed only after Australia's captain Greg Chappell persuaded Lillee to use a conventional bat. Lillee acquiesced reluctantly as he threw the offending bat twenty yards in anger. After this incident, cricket's lawmakers amended the rules immediately, adding a clause that bats must be made of wood.

LILLEE AND MIANDAD GET PHYSICAL

This incident was at the same venue but two years later. Lillee was fined and suspended for 2 one-day internationals after aiming a kick at the Pakistan captain Javed Miandad on the fourth day of the first Test in Perth in November 1981, as according to him, the Pakistani had used swear words at him. Observed Ken Piesse in *Cricket's Greatest Scandals* (2001), Miandad menacingly brandished his bat in retaliation. Not to be outdone, Lillee clenched his fists and shaped up like an old-time bare-knuckle boxer as the commentators and spectators held their breath. From slip skipper Greg Chappell yelled 'Dennis!' and rushed down the pitch to intervene. Umpire Tony Crafter had to separate combatants Miandad and Lillee.

Miandad later explained, 'I lifted my bat to ward him off and to tell him that if he hit me, I'd hit him for saying dirty words to me.' Somehow it seemed unfair that although Lillee received the punishment he deserved, Miandad walked free.

Lillee wrote in his book *Over and Out* (1984) that this was the only on-field controversy he truly regretted:

> Javed jabbed me in the rib cage with his bat, but nobody wanted to know about it. I'm not saying I was right in what I did, even though I gave him only a slight tap on the field. I'm sorry thousands of kids saw it, but I'm also sorry the incident wasn't fully shown in television replays.

500/1 BET IS ON

The Ashes Test at Headingly, Leeds, in July 1981 remains one of the most amazing in Test history. It was the third Test in the series, Australia was leading 1–0 and sailing smoothly to a certain 2–0 lead. What other result can be possible with England following on 227 runs behind and being 4 for 42 and then 7 for 135 in the second innings on the fourth day? They were still 92 runs in arrears with their top seven batsmen gone, only all-rounder Ian Botham and the tail-enders remaining between Kim Hughes' Australians and an innings victory.

To arouse some interest in the one–sided match, betting agency Ladbrokes offered the extraordinary odds of 500 to 1 on a series–levelling English win. The local Yorkshiremen ignored these absurd odds thinking that the match would end on the fourth day. However, in the Australian dressing room, Lillee could not believe his ears. He somehow convinced wicketkeeper Rod Marsh, and the two put money on the incredible chance of England winning. They thought it was a giggle bet.

As Botham later wrote in *The Incredible Tests* 1981 (1982), 'Most of us had given up the Test for dead.' But how he resuscitated the dead match is part of cricketing folklore. After top–scoring with 50 in England's first innings of 174, 'Beefy' Botham hit a magnificent and unbeaten 149 in the second, adding 117 runs with tailender Graham Dilley (56) and 67 with Chris Old (29). The home team had made an astonishing rally to total 356, the last three wickets adding 221 runs. Still, Australia needed only 130 to win and was at one stage one for 56, just 74 runs needed with nine wickets intact. A cakewalk, surely!

To arouse some interest in the one–sided match, betting agency Ladbrokes offered the extraordinary odds of 500 to 1 on a series–levelling English win. The local Yorkshiremen ignored these absurd odds thinking that the match would end on the fourth day.

But tall English paceman Bob Willis was not convinced. He captured 8 for 43 and Australia collapsed for 111 (losing 9 for 55) and England won by 18 runs. The Australians were devastated.

While there were rumours of a bet by Lillee and Marsh, details remained in-house until Lillee's autobiography *My Life in Cricket* (1982) was published a year later. In it, Lillee frankly wrote about the wager. The Australian Cricket Board (now Cricket Australia) was embarrassed and immediately inserted a clause into the players' contracts, banning players from betting.

As Piesse quotes Lillee in *Cricket's Greatest Scandals* (2001):

I never lost a moment's sleep because of it. I didn't regard it as betting against my team or my country. I have a completely clear conscience over it ... I believe my integrity, as far as playing to win every game I play, is unquestioned.

Marsh said that both he and Lillee felt they were betting against the English bookmakers, trying to demonstrate to them how silly they were to offer such stupid odds of 500/1. He added, 'I could not see the harm in having a bet. Nobody would have cared if we had won ... I don't believe we did the wrong thing because we did not consider it a bet against Australia.'

Lillee was more emphatic. 'I'd flatten anyone who ever suggested I threw a game.' However, former Australian great batsman Neil Harvey was not convinced. According to him, Lillee should have been banned from cricket.

[18]
SUNNY GAVASKAR'S
RUNS AND
RUN-INS

ndia's legendary opening batsman Sunil 'Sunny' Gavaskar is remembered for his runs. He is the first batsman to score 10 000 runs in Test arena; mostly against the most intimidating fast bowling attacks, the West Indies speed quartet of Andy Roberts, Michael Holding, Joe Garner and Malcolm Marshall; the Aussie fearsome two-some of Dennis Lillee and Jeff Thomson; John Snow from England, Imran Khan from Pakistan ... And without using a proper helmet!

But he is also remembered for his run-ins with authorities, umpires and opposing cricketers.

I was batting well for the first time in the series I was middling the ball well. It looked like I would get a few runs when a ball from Lillee kept low and as I played it with the inside edge of the bat it went on to hit the pad. After that, a typical Lillee appeal for leg before wicket followed as he danced down the track, eventually winning the appeal.

The 21-year old, 165 cm short, Sunny announced his arrival to the Test scene in 1971 in the West Indies by scoring 774 runs at 154.80 in four Tests, a record for a debutant in Test history. This is how he thrashed the Windies attack; 65 and 67 not out in his Test debut at Port-of-Spain as India gained her first win against the Garry Sobers-led Windies, followed by tall scores of 116 and 64 not out, 1 and 117 not out, 124 and 220 in successive innings. He became the second cricketer after Australia's Doug Walters to register a century and a double century in the same Test. Remarkably, Gavaskar's century and double century in the same Test in Port-of-Spain had come in his initial Test series.

He retired from Test cricket in 1986, hitting 34 centuries, then a record, and contributed handsomely to a few Test wins for India as well. His illustrious career was full of milestones. But this book is on controversies and not on landmarks and he is not a stranger to them either.

The biggest controversy in his career came in the much-discussed Melbourne Test of February 1981. Leading 1-0 in the 3-Test series, Australia needed only 143 runs to win this Test and the series 2-0. But on a crumbling MCG pitch, Greg Chappell's team collapsed for 83 to lose by 59 runs, India's all-rounder Kapil Dev captured 5 for 28 despite a pulled thigh muscle. But the match is more remembered for the Gavaskar 'pull out' incident on the fourth day, 10 February.

Trailing Australia by 182 runs, India put up a big fight in the second innings; skipper Gavaskar and Chetan Chauhan putting on 165 runs for the opening wicket. Both the Indian openers were playing comfortably on a wicket with plenty of juice when it happened. When 70, Gavaskar was given out lbw to Dennis Lillee. Gavaskar vehemently disagreed with this decision and openly argued with umpire Rex Whitehead. On hearing sledges from the bowler, Gavaskar lost his cool and urged his partner Chauhan to leave the field with him. Thus India had come close to forfeiting this match.

Fortunately, for India and for cricket, India's manager Wing Commander S.K. Durrani met the pair at the gate and ordered Chauhan to continue his innings. Although Gavaskar is my friend and a hero, he was wrong in doing what he did in the Melbourne Test.

Here is how Gavaskar explains the background of the above incident in his book *Idols* (1983):

I was batting well for the first time in the series I was middling the ball well. It looked like I would get a few runs when a ball from Lillee kept low and as I played it with the inside edge of the bat it went on to hit the pad. After that, a typical Lillee appeal for leg before wicket followed as he danced down the track, eventually winning the appeal. At this stage I must say that the umpiring of Mr Whitehead had disappointed us, for he gave a lot of decisions that went against us.

Gavaskar added that it was going to a stage that his teammates were requesting him that he should do something about it. 'For example,' he disclosed, 'the previous day when Allan Border was bowled when trying to sweep Shivlal Yadav, the umpires had to confer with each other to give that decision.'

After that, wicketkeeper Syed Kirmani told Gavaskar that if the umpire had given Border not out he would have walked out. Perhaps that word 'walk out' was subconsciously imprinted on his mind so the next day when Lillee's appeal was upheld he was furious against the umpire for giving that decision. Gavaskar continued:

When the umpire did not reverse his decision a lot of anger was boiling within me but still the idea of walking off did not strike me. When I walked past Chetan, I heard friend Lillee utter one of his profanities which was a very delayed reaction from him and it was then that I lost my balance of mind and told Chetan to walk off with me. That is one of the most regrettable incidents in my life. Whatever may be the provocation and whatever the reason, there was no justification for my action and now I realise that I did not behave the way a captain and sportsman should. I take all blame and responsibility for my action... I do not fully blame Lillee because whatever may be the provocation, I should have kept my cool and allowed the anger to die down.

Far from feeling chastised, Snow sent a message to the English selection hierarchy, 'Tell them they can stuff themselves.' Earlier, Snow was feeling pleased with himself in the above Test, having top-scored for England with 73, his highest score in first-class cricket.

Lillee later apologised for his action.

He still maintains that he had played the ball and was not out. However, Dennis Lillee in his book *Over and Out* (1984) claimed that Gavaskar had not played the ball at all and was clearly out.

This on-field altercation has not altered Gavaskar's opinion of Lillee. According to him, 'Dennis Lillee is the greatest fast bowler in cricketing history.'

A decade before the MCG 1981 near walk-out, Gavaskar had a run-in with England's fast bowler John Snow, the incident now remembered as 'Snow's Sunny charge'. Snow was suspended for a Test after shouldering Gavaskar in the first Test at Lord's in July 1971.

Far from feeling chastised, Snow sent a message to the English selection hierarchy, 'Tell them they can stuff themselves.' Earlier, Snow was feeling pleased with himself in the above Test, having top-scored for England with 73, his highest score in first-class cricket. Needing 183 for a win, Gavaskar made 53 but Snow collided with him when the latter was completing a quick single. Rain prevented India from winning their first Test in England when 38 runs short and two wickets in hand.

Sunny Gavaskar recalls this incident in his book *Sunny Days* (1976):

Earlier, during our partnership [with Farokh Engineer], just before lunch, an incident, the famous 'Snow charge', took place involving me. Snow bowled to Farokh from the Nursery End, and Farokh trying to turn the ball to leg missed and was hit on the thigh and the ball fell near short square-leg. We set off for a quick run. From the corner of the eye I saw Snow also setting off for the ball. I would have reached 'home' safely as Snow had gone across to the other side of his follow through.

However, I found to my surprise that he was level with me and, with the ball nowhere near him, the hefty fast bowler gave me a violent shove, which sent me sprawling.

As Snow is well built, 'shorty' Gavaskar had no chance. He crawled back to the crease having lost the bat. 'Snow came and tossed the bat back to me. He did not fling it as reported in the newspapers. In fact, after lunch he came to me and apologised', Gavaskar explained.

DESPITE HIS LOVE HATE RELATIONS WITH Australia, Sunil Gavaskar became the first non-Australian to be recognised as Bradman Honouree at the Don Bradman Gala Dinner hosted at the Sydney Cricket Ground in October 2010. This Award was established in 2006 to recognise players who played the game well and faithfully in line with Sir Donald Bradman's values. The previous honourees were all Australians: Norman O'Neill in 2006, Neil Harvey and Sam Loxton in 2007, Bill Brown and Arthur Morris in 2008 and Alan Davidson and Dennis Lillee in 2009. In 2010, Gavaskar shared this honour with Adam Glchrist.

Embodying the Bradman principles of courage, honour and integrity, Gavaskar had a profound impact on cricket in India and the world. He is recognised as one of the most successful of all opening batsmen and is credited for teaching his teammates and their successors the virtue of unconditional professionalism.

He also taught them to fight fire with fire and not let bullies prosper, although he went too far on a few occasions. The brave new India owes a lot to him.

CHUCKING
ROW I — MECKIFF
AND EGAR

Mention the word 'chucking' and a majority will think about Sri Lankan unorthodox off-spinner Muttiah Muralitharan and Australian umpire Darrell Hair in the 1995 Melbourne Test. Actually, chucking or throwing was with us long before that. The first cricketer to be called for no-balling was Australia's fast bowler Ernie Jones against England in the Melbourne Test of January 1898. He was no-balled by Australian umpire Jim Phillips.

Since then: England's Tony Lock against West Indies at Jamaica in 1953-54, South Africa's Geoff Griffin against England at Lord's in 1960, and Pakistan's Haseeb Ahsan against India in Bombay in 1960-61 are among others who have been called by umpires for chucking in a Test match.

A major controversy erupted when Australian fast bowler Ian Meckiff, from Victoria, was no-balled. Not once, not twice but four times in his only over in the first Test of the 1963 Brisbane Test against South Africa by South Australian umpire Colin Egar, standing at square-leg. This was the end of Meckiff's Test career as he retired from all cricket, having taken 45 wickets at 31.62 in eighteen Tests. The slim but sinewy left-arm quickie was then only 28 years old. He even refused to play social matches lest someone would yell the hateful word 'chucker'.

From a casual run of sixteen paces, and with a left arm disconcertingly bent, Meckiff bowled fast amid unending controversy for almost 8 first-class seasons, until umpire Egar wrote a finish to his career on Saturday 7 December 1963, in the Brisbane Test. Some found this instant ending of a Test career tragic, others considered that justice was finally done. His action had been an object of suspicion since the 1958-59 Ashes series, when his 6 for 38 in the second innings of the second Test in Melbourne included the scalps of classy batsmen Peter May, Colin Cowdrey and Tom Graveney.

Meckiff was outlawed for almost three years for a suspect action caused by a permanently bent left arm. This genial and good-natured cricketer was depicted by a reporter on the Melbourne *Herald's* London staff 'as the greatest ogre of international cricket since Larwood'.

In his book *Thrown Out* (1961), Meckiff proclaimed his innocence. He admitted that his wristy front-on action may not have been as pure as some, but any jerkiness was only an optical illusion. He wrote angrily, 'But the one reason I find it hard to fill the bill as a ferocious cheat is one the critics chose to ignore—I DO NOT THROW THE BALL!'

He starts his autobiography with a hyperbole of sarcasm in response to his being labelled the greatest ogre of international cricket since Larwood:

Ian Meckiff is 10 feet tall, bowls at 3000 miles an hour, and tries to kill batsmen ... It's doubtful if any player has been such a profitable source of income for cricket writers than me. There's little I haven't been called. They accused me of throwing every ball, of bowling Bodyline, of throwing England out on the 1958–59 tour of Australia, of causing the game to degenerate, of causing a rift in the relations between the Australian Board of Control and the MCC, and of being 'King' of the world's chuckers.

Probably the reason other umpires did not no–ball them for chucking at Test level was because they did not want to get embroiled in a major controversy. However, in the 1962–63 season, Meckiff was no–balled twice in Sheffield Shield matches.

Johnny Wardle, the former English Test spinner, accused Meckiff of 'throwing England out'.

Meckiff added that he had been passed in all major cricket–playing countries (Australia, South Africa, New Zealand, India and Pakistan) before umpire Egar rocked his boat. Muralitharan put forward the same argument three decades later against Australian umpires (see the next chapter). Probably the reason other umpires did not no–ball them for chucking at Test level was because they did not want to get embroiled in a major controversy. However, in the 1962–63 season, Meckiff was no–balled twice in Sheffield Shield matches.

After being out of international cricket for a few years, Meckiff was delighted at his shock recall to the Australian team for the Brisbane Test in 1963. But soon it turned to horror after his second, third, fifth and ninth deliveries of his only over in that Test were no–balled by umpire Egar.

Now let's look at this incident from the umpire's point of view. When Egar no–balled Meckiff, he must have anticipated ramifications. But he had strong beliefs and the courage of his convictions. As Australia's senior umpire, he reckoned he had a responsibility to act. He said, 'Let's face it, somebody had to do something.'

As Ken Piesse wrote in *Cricket's Greatest Scandals* (2001), 'He [Egar] said he could have called more often but then the over would never have finished.'

So did Meckiff chuck? Many thought he was made a scapegoat of a purge and even today after almost 50 years there is an uneasy silence surrounding the Meckiff–Egar saga. There were contrasting viewpoints even among Australian cricketers past and present. For Simpson, there was no doubt that he chucked. But not according to Ian Redpath, Bill Lawry and selector Jack Ryder.

Redpath commented, 'I'd never say that "Meck" was a chucker. He was perhaps stiff.' He added that Meckiff was a genuine in–swing bowler who hit the pitch hard. 'It's a very difficult thing to do; throw a ball and swing it the same time.'

When Meckiff said there was a type of conspiracy against him in the selection, I thought he was overreacting or getting paranoid. But after doing some research into this 'throwma' (a new word coined by me to describe the throwing drama), I have second thoughts.

Eleven months before the no–balling of Meckiff by Egar, a frame–by–frame film of Meckiff's action was shown at Sir Donald Bradman's home. This happened a few days before the January 1963 Ashes Test in Adelaide.

Eleven months before the no–balling of Meckiff by Egar, a frame–by–frame film of Meckiff's action was shown at Sir Donald Bradman's home. This happened a few days before the January 1963 Ashes Test in Adelaide. Bradman held a dinner at his home in Kensington where he invited State captains Richie Benaud, Bill Lawry, Barry Shepherd and Ken Mackay, among others. After the dinner he showed some interesting films on bowlers with suspect actions including a frame–by–frame film of Meckiff. The case against Meckiff was damning, even with his 'new' action.

Both Lawry and Ryder, who were pro–Meckiff, changed their viewpoint after watching the film. Lawry said, 'But that evening ... a camera showed that Ian Meckiff bent his left arm at the point of delivery.' In what amounted to the first emphatic use of video film technology in Australian cricket, it was clear that when slowed down, Meckiff's action was illegal.

Test captain Benaud's reaction was prompt, he wrote in *Anything but ... An Autobiography* (1998):

At the end of the evening I said that, in future, I would not continue to bowl anyone called for throwing by an umpire, and I intended to go a step further, as I had done in Sydney a few days earlier, and not continue to bowl anyone in my team I considered to have a suspect action.

Yet eleven months later, he captained an Australian Test team that included Meckiff who was no-balled twice in Sheffield Shield matches that season and whose action had been suspected by none other than Bradman who was a national selector. Was it a turnaround in thinking?

Questions were also raised as to why Benaud had not bowled Meckiff from the other end where Lou Rowan and not Egar would be standing at square-leg. The Brisbane crowd was supportive of Meckiff and wanted Benaud to do exactly that. They booed and jeered the captain and chanted 'We want Meckiff'.

Benaud explained in *Anything but ... An Autobiography* that 'the selectors would nominate the side and they would make sure the bowlers in the team were completely legitimate–my job was simply to captain ...'

Questions were also raised as to why Benaud had not bowled Meckiff from the other end where Lou Rowan and not Egar would be standing at square-leg. The Brisbane crowd was supportive of Meckiff and wanted Benaud to do exactly that. They booed and jeered the captain, and chanted 'We want Meckiff'.

Benaud explained that in accordance with his stated policy he would not bowl a bowler once called by an umpire in a match and Meckiff now fell in that category. As Mark Browning wrote in *Richie Benaud — Cricketer, Captain, Guru* (1996), 'The other umpire, Lou Rowan, later said he would have called Meckiff for throwing if Benaud had tried to bring him at the other end.'

Was the selection of Meckiff in the December 1963 Brisbane Test a sort of conspiracy? Dubbed as 'Meckiff's Test' by the Australian media, speculation was rife that the Victorian quickie was selected so he could be no-balled as a public relations debate to demonstrate worldwide Australia's anti–throwing campaign. The legendary Australian all–rounder Keith Miller described Meckiff's selection to pepper 'this drab–looking series into a curry hot–pot, with all the excitement and trimmings of an Alfred Hitchcock thriller'. Another former Test great, Bill O'Reilly, wrote in the *Sydney Morning Herald* that the selection of Meckiff was 'one of the most fantastic somersaults in cricket policies of our time'.

Now spare a thought for umpire Col Egar, a friend of Meckiff and his partner in lawn bowls. Horns of dilemma for Col! Why was Meckiff selected when the selectors and the captain knew that he had a suspect action? Why was he publicly humiliated?

Now spare a thought for umpire Col Egar, a friend of Meckiff and his partner in lawn bowls. Horns of dilemma for Col! Why was Meckiff selected when the selectors and the captain knew that he had a suspect action? Why was he publicly humiliated?

The controversy and speculations apart, it was a happy Test for Benaud. He took 5 for 68 and scored 43 runs in the first innings to become the first cricketer to reach the Test double of 2000 runs and 200 wickets.

However, this was the last Test Benaud captained as he was injured soon after when playing a Sydney first grade match for Cumberland against Mosman at Mosman Oval. He recalled, 'In trying to take a catch off Doug Walters' bowling at third slip early in the morning, I broke in three places the third finger of my bowling hand—my spinning finger. I looked down at my hand and said, "Would you bloody well believe it?" ' Bob Simpson took over as Australia's captain although Benaud played three more Tests in the series.

Chucking has always remained an enormously emotional issue. Simpson, former Australian opening batsman, captain and coach, calls it an insidious evil and recommended that all chuckers be thrown out of the game. It should be remembered that India's captain and opening batsman, Nari Contractor, almost died from a skull fracture after ducking into a lightning fast delivery from West Indian quickie Charlie Griffith in a match against Barbados in 1962. Later, Griffith was nicknamed 'Charlie the chucker'.

In his autobiography *Captain's Story* (1966), Simpson was very critical of

Meckiff's mode of bowling, referring to his action as 'throwing at his spectacular best'. As a result of a court case, publisher Stanley Paul withdrew the book. It was released as a paperback in 1977 where the chapter on Meckiff was deleted. It seems paradoxical that if Meckiff was so sensitive about being called a chucker why on the cover of his 1961 autobiography *Thrown Out*, the author's name was given as Ian 'Chucker' Meckiff? He was probably chucking a beamer at his critics!

However, in the paperback edition of *Captain's Story* a chapter on West Indies express fast bowler Griffith was retained. Simpson labelled him a chucker as he vividly described the first Test at Jamaica in March 1965:

Then it happened. Charlie lay back his powerful frame to generate the fury of a typhoon. The ball, a screaming yorker as fast as any I have seen, thudded into the turf near me before I had time to move. It had taken just one ball and I knew: Charlie Griffith is a chucker. No man can project a ball at ninety miles an hour from almost a standing start without throwing it.

Although Griffith was no-balled in first-class matches in 1961–62 and in 1966, he was never no-balled in any of his 28 Tests. One may ask why?

BILL LAWRY WAS A PRANKSTER. WHEN sharing a room with Richie Benaud on tours, he would play practical jokes on his immaculate roommate. Like nailing down Richie's slippers at night making him take an early morning tumble, shouting, 'That bloody Lawry!'

But Lawry went a step further during the controversial 'Meckiff Test'. Earlier on the day the Gabba crowd had jeered the Aussie captain when he did not make Meckiff bowl at the other end and for which Melbourne's *Sporting Globe* had written a scathing article. Lawry, in one of his more elaborate jokes, set up Jock, the masseur, to front Benaud with the newspaper *Globe* covering a gun and saying, 'I'm a Meckiff fan'. Soon he whipped away the newspaper, pointed the gun at Benaud and then fired. Recalls Benaud in his *Anything but … An Autobiography*, 'It wasn't quite a heart-stopper, but it was close for a moment or two until I realised it was a cap-gun!' It must be the first and only time that Richie lost his cool. Marvellous. We can imagine Lawry going high-pitched: 'Got him!'

[20]
CHUCKING
ROW II — MURALI
AND HAIR

A major event is one that you can remember as to exactly where you were when it happened. Like Australia's victory in America's Cup in 1983 or Cathy Freeman winning the sprinting race in the 2000 Sydney Olympics or umpire Darrell Hair no-balling Muttiah Muralitharan in the 1995 Boxing Day Melbourne Test.

I had just finished a sumptuous luncheon at a friend's Boxing Day party. While others were enjoying a swim or dancing, or watching the Sydney–Hobart yacht race from the balcony of the waterfront property, I hid myself in the hosts' TV room, surreptitiously watching the Boxing Day Australia–Sri Lanka Test with the sound switched on mute. I did not want to appear as a party-pooper! Like the 55,239 spectators on the opening day at the MCG, I was enjoying the batting of Michael Slater and David Boon against some keen Sri Lankan bowling when *it* happened. And commentators, journalists, cricket followers have not stopped talking about that dramatic afternoon since then.

The Australian umpire, Hair, no-balled Sri Lanka's unconventional off-spinner Muralitharan seven times in three overs. As he made his judgement from the bowler's end, several minutes passed before I realised that it was Murali's elbow rather than his foot landing that was at fault. To quote *Wisden* 1997, 'Many were unimpressed. Former Australian fast bowler, Ian Meckiff—who retired after being called in Brisbane in 1963—was so affected that he went home.'

That had been the procedure followed during a tournament in Sharjah where Murali had been playing and where he was the subject of a discussion between Hair, Dunne, English umpire Nigel Plews and match referee Raman Subba Row (who had previously played 13 Tests for England).

Skipper Arjuna Ranatunga made Murali switch ends and bowled unchanged without any no-ball calls from the New Zealand umpire Steve Dunne. Then Hair told Ranatunga that he was ready to call him from square-leg.

In his book *Alone in the Middle: An Umpire's Story* (2003), Dunne tells his version of the above episode, as quoted in *Cricinfo* by Lynn McConnell. Dunne was standing at square-leg when Muralitharan came on to bowl and was called for no-balls by Australian umpire

Hair. Then the latter walked across to Dunne and told him, 'Those no-balls were not for foot faults.'

Dunne described the mounting tension and said in hindsight his view was, 'Here was a cricket controversy of the first magnitude.' Ranatunga left the field and then came out and put Muralitharan on at Dunne's end.

'The atmosphere was electric,' said Dunne, the first to umpire 100 one-day internationals:

> When spinners bowled, my method had always been to stand as close to the stumps as possible, because the closer you got the more likely you were to be able to pick up a bat-pad nick. I would have got a better view of Muralitharan's arm by standing back, but I elected not to change the habit I had formed—and which had served me well—during my umpiring career.
>
> There were many thoughts going through my mind. What do I do? Do I support Hair because he has called Muralitharan and do I call him as well? Or do I support what I believe, which was what we had discussed and decided at a conference in Coventry earlier this year?

That conference had decided in the case of a suspect action that the matter would be reported to the match referee who would have the action filmed and sent to the International Cricket Council.

That had been the procedure followed during a tournament in Sharjah where Murali had been playing and where he was the subject of a discussion between Hair, Dunne, English umpire Nigel Plews and match referee Raman Subba Row (who had previously played 13 Tests for England).

'Nigel, Darrell and I were unanimous in our belief that Muralitharan had a problem,' Dunne wrote:

> We told Dav Whatmore [coach] what we'd done and said that Sri Lanka should take remedial action because Muralitharan could have problems down the track. The short answer was that, during that dramatic day in Melbourne, I stuck to what had been agreed on and did not call him. The atmosphere between Darrell and me when we returned to the dressing room at stumps was, needless to say, cool. I have great respect for Darrell as an umpire and person. He is someone I've always got on very well with and still do.

Dunne believed that by calling a player for throwing was virtually saying he couldn't play the game, and that was too 'Godlike'. He said he came under pressure from the media for not backing Hair up, but he countered by believing he had done the right thing.

As I said before, I don't believe it's possible to do so with the naked eye and I wouldn't want to play God. But I would report him to the match referee on suspicion that his action might not be fair. He is a unique bowler, in more ways than one and I suspect that problems he poses both to officialdom and opposition batsmen won't go away.

'My argument was that he had played in about 30 Tests at the time, he had been watched by numerous umpires, and only one had called him', continued Dunne. 'They were now telling me I was wrong by not supporting that one and disagreeing with the others.'

Dunne wrote that at the end of the match, the match referee, New Zealander Graham Dowling, had called him into his hotel room and asked why he hadn't called Muralitharan for throwing ... I still wouldn't call Muralitharan for throwing if I was umpiring him today:

As I said before, I don't believe it's possible to do so with the naked eye and I wouldn't want to play God. But I would report him to the match referee on suspicion that his action might not be fair. He is a unique bowler, in more ways than one and I suspect that problems he poses both to officialdom and opposition batsmen won't go away. They lie in the too-hard basket. It is not his fault, but he has caused more arguments than any player of the past decade.

Hair's version is quite the contrary. As he explained in 3-dimensional details in his free-hitting autobiography *Decision Maker – An Umpire's Story* (1998):

Muralidharan (sic) came on to bowl from my end mid-way between lunch and tea ... Initially he bowled with a bent arm which I believe is perfectly legal. As he warmed up and attempted to impart more spin, the arm straightened fractionally, and progressively becoming more definitely 'illegal'.

Hair struggled to find a solution and thought of mentioning this to skipper Arjuna Ranatunga with a request that he withdrew Murali from the attack. But he thought better of it as this was a Test match and doubted whether such conversation should take place, let alone work. He continued:

History now records that I called Muralidharan (sic) seven times during the next three overs ... In reality I could have called him twenty seven times or even more. I did not want the matter to become a complete farce as I was certain his captain would simply remove him from the attack. Arjuna left the field, consulted with team management, and returned with the remarkable decision that he would bowl Muralidharan from the other end.

This was quite contrary to how Richie Benaud had acted in the Brisbane Test of 1963. As described in the previous chapter, Benaud did not bowl Ian Meckiff from the other end once Colin Egar had no-balled him from square-leg.

This put additional pressure on umpire Dunne in the MCG 1995 Boxing Day Test. Dunne's version is already given. But Hair was not happy. During the tea break he spoke to the ICC match referee, Graham Dowling, and pleaded with him to request the Sri Lankan management to instruct Ranatunga not to bowl Murali again. But the referee did not agree with Hair. And the rest is history.

Next day's newspapers carried headlines on the Hair—Murali—Ranatunga saga with all three coming under strong criticism. Hair recalled, 'The media hysteria was manageable but I was terrified when I received death threats delivered to my home through the mail, even placed in my letterbox without stamps.'

The relations between Australia and Sri Lanka had started on the wrong foot a fortnight earlier on 9 December in the first Test at Perth. Umpires Khizar Hayat from Pakistan and Peter Parker of Queensland decided that someone in Sri Lanka's attack had tampered with the seam of the ball. The touring team protested vehemently.

The umpires had erred in not impounding the ball so there really was no evidence. Match referee Dowling also erred in believing the umpires without proof of the ball being 'doctored' and without listening to the Sri Lankan's story. They became the first team convicted of ball-tampering in a Test but the ICC reversed the finding a fortnight later.

The controversies kept piling on. It deteriorated further when Murali dropped out of the team after being called again for throwing. Peace talks were held at the Australian Cricket Board where umpire Hair denied that he had made racist remarks to the Sri Lankans and explained that he had addressed them as 'you blokes'. To quote Trent Bouts from *Wisden* 1997, 'It was a season of crossed wires as much as crossed swords and rancour continued into the last match at Sydney.'

This happened in the second Benson and Hedges World Series Final in Sydney on 20 January, 1996, three weeks after the Boxing Day saga. Australia's series win was marred by an earlier on-field verbal stoush between wicketkeeper Ian Healy and Ranatunga. At the presentation ceremony some visitors refused to shake Australian captain Mark Taylor's hand. Healy made unpleasant remarks to Sri Lankan coach Dav Whatmore for which he later apologised.

This explosive and acrimonious series in Australia was soon followed by the 1996 World Cup in India, Pakistan and Sri Lanka. And there were controversies before a ball was bowled. The bomb blasts in Colombo, Sri Lanka, a fortnight before the World Cup, made Australia and the West Indies, refuse to play their group matches in Colombo for security reasons and they forfeited these games. Despite this, Australia entered the Final. The venue was Lahore, Pakistan, and their opponents were none other than Sri Lanka under Ranatunga. Playing with fire and vengeance, Sri Lanka won comfortably by seven wickets and with 22 balls in hand to lift their one and only World Cup. The stylish Aravinda de Silva scored a brilliant 107 not out and added 97 runs with Ranatunga.

No one could wipe the smile of satisfaction from Ranatunga's face for days!

But the conflict between Murali and Australian umpires was reignited when Sri Lanka toured Australia for a tri-nation Carlton & United one-day international (ODI) series in 1998–99. It was tension all over again when Australian umpire Ross Emerson no-balled Murali in the match against England in an ODI at Adelaide on 23 January 1999. This was one of the most heated and controversial ODIs ever played.

The 'throwma' (throwing drama) started when Murali, in his second over, was called for throwing by square-leg umpire Emerson. In rage, skipper Ranatunga led his men towards the boundary and the match was halted for 14 minutes as the Sri Lankan management spoke to their Cricket Board in Colombo on a mobile phone.

The visitors were ordered to go back to the pitch but the on-field dispute continued. When Ranatunga insisted that Emerson should stand closer to the stumps as Murali (who had switched ends) was bowling, many felt that Ranatunga was the villain—how dare he tell an accredited umpire where to stand. However, Emerson also came in for criticism for pursuing his own agenda when ICC had specifically cleared Murali's action.

The drama went on as England's captain and wicketkeeper Alec Stewart was overheard by television microphones telling Ranatunga, 'Your behaviour today has been appalling for a country captain.' Despite all these trauma and tantrums, Sri Lankan batsmen kept their heads, chasing 303 with one wicket and two balls in hand. And who hit the winning runs? Murali!

The stylish Aravinda de Silva scored a brilliant 107 not out and added 97 runs with Ranatunga. No one could wipe the smile of satisfaction from Ranatunga's face for days!

Often the only Tamil in the side in a time of ethnic conflict, Murali became as powerful a unifying force as any in the country. The civil war in the country was forgotten as all Sri Lankans rallied round Murali. Backed to the hilt by his skipper Ranatunga, Murali blossomed in his career, which had as many snakes as ladders.

Muralitharan may not be every purist's cup of tea but I cannot end this chapter without paying a tribute to perhaps the most controversial cricketer, even more controversial than Douglas Jardine. Murali is the most prolific wicket-taker in Test annals, the only bowler to capture 800 wickets—his landmark 800th scalp came off his final ball in Test when he claimed the wicket of India's Pragyan Ojha at Galle on 22 July 2010. Not poetry in motion as say Shane Warne was, he bowled in free verse confounding the best batsmen with his off-spin, doosras (a leg-break with an off-break action) and unorthodoxy.

Murali was allowed to bowl later in his career because the ICC effectively changed the rules, allowing bowlers to straighten their arm by up to 15 degrees of tolerance during their delivery.

He had as many admirers as an exceptional bowler as he had doubters who thought he was responsible for legitimising chucking by the less than 15 degrees arm-straightening escape clause. In his defence it must be stated that he was born with a deformed elbow and was double-jointed. But according to Hair, 'Not that he [Murali] throws all the time. He is quite capable of bowling legally when he wants to.'

Simon Barnes in *Wisden* 2007 paid Muralitharan this tribute:

There are people who will continue to express reservations. They are a familiar type: sneerers and begrudgers, the pusillanimous possessors of small minds and large opinions. Muralitharan is a truly great cricketer, and those who cannot go along with such a sentiment have something lacking in their souls. The spirit of cricket, perhaps.

Murali had marvellous achievements as a bowler at both Test and ODI levels, but the one he will cherish most was when the Australia-Sri Lanka Test series was named The Warne-Muralitharan Trophy in 2007.

THE GATTING–SHAKOOR FINGER–
POINTING IN FAISALABAD

The Faisalabad Test between Pakistan and England in December 1987 was among the most acrimonious matches ever played with allegations and counter allegations of verbal abuse, cheating and a threat of strike action by the English players.

The finger–pointing between England's captain Mike Gatting and Pakistan umpire Shakoor Rana will be discussed for a long time. Shakoor came face-to-face with Gatting in the finger–waving episode that literally stopped the Test for a day as telegrams were exchanged between the English team, the Pakistan Cricket Board and the Test and County Cricket Board (TCCB) at Lord's. The sight of the England captain and an international umpire shouting at each other with fingers waved in each other's face was a shocking one for the reputation of the game.

With Pakistan struggling at 5 for 106 and still 186 behind England's first innings total of 292, square–leg umpire Shakoor invoked Law 42 on the grounds of unfair play by Gatting. The England captain had informed batsman Salim Malik and then moved fielder David Capel as off–spinner Eddie Hemmings ran in to bowl. Shakoor stopped the game and accused Gatting of cheating. Gatting denied this accusation.

Before this explosive incident, Shakoor had upset the English team by wearing a Pakistan sweater and placing Mudassar Nazar's cap on his own head.

The game was stopped as both Shakoor and Gatting accused each other of using foul language, much of which was heard by a worldwide television audience via the stump camera. It was not until the next day that the full magnitude of the spat became clear.

Shakoor refused to stand in that Test until he received an unconditional apology from Gatting for the language used in the dispute and Gatting refused to apologise unless the umpire reciprocated. Negotiations continued through the night and into the rest of the day. England's tour manager Peter Lush's indefatigable attempts to resolve the impasse were frustrated by the Pakistani officials.

Gatting was threatened with being stripped of the England captaincy and was forced into issuing a written apology to Shakoor by the management. The players threatened to refuse to play if their captain received instructions to write an apology. But when the instructions came and Gatting wrote a brief apology to Shakoor, they decided to continue playing under protest. However, they insisted that umpire Shakoor was the first to use abusive language to Gatting.

In a strongly worded statement, the players stated, 'The incident was sad for cricket but the solution forced upon us was sadder.'

After the tour it was learnt that Gatting had received a letter from Shakoor during the next Test in Karachi a week later. It was not made public because, according to the captain, it was an expression of regret rather than an apology.

It was made public a few months later that each England player was secretly paid £1000 as 'hardship bonus'. When it came out in the open, the TCCB, according to *Wisden* 1989, was badly placed to fend off allegations that the money had been awarded either by way of a 'bribe' to save the tour or as 'conscience money' for its poor handling of the affair.

The tour went ahead, the controversy–laden Test was drawn and Pakistan won the series 1–0.

MIKE GATTING WAS NOT THE ONLY international captain to have had a run–in with Shakoor Rana. In the December 1984 Karachi Test, New Zealand captain Jeremy Coney threatened to lead his side from the field following a controversial decision when Pakistan's legendary batsman Javed Miandad was given not out after wicketkeeper Ian Smith had caught him.

England's wicketkeeper Alan Knott has mixed feelings for his innings in the Karachi Test of March 1969 against Pakistan. He needed only four runs for his first Test hundred but could not reach it. Was he out? Did he run out of partners? Neither. Rioting forced the organisers to abandon the match with England on 7 for 502 and Knott on 96 not out.

[22]
THE MANY
SPLENDOURED
DEANO

Mention the name Dean Jones to ten cricket enthusiasts and all ten will immediately remember his epic double century in the tied Test between Australia and India in Madras (now Chennai) in September 1986. He had batted for almost eight and a half hours in scorching heat to score a gallant 210 with 27 fours and two sixes. He battled nausea and leg cramps. Soon after he was hospitalised and treated for dehydration.

About seven out of ten will remember his gaffe of thoughtlessly and unintentionally calling South Africa's bearded Muslim batsman, Hashim Amla, a terrorist when commentating on television. This was during the fourth day's play between Sri Lanka and South Africa at Colombo in August 2006. I will discuss this in more detail later.

But few will remember his bizarre run out in the Guyana Test between Australia and the West Indies in March 1991. Trailing the Windies by 221 runs in the first innings, 'Deano' Jones came to the wicket in a crisis at 3 for 67. Then it happened. He was 'bowled' off a no-ball by Courtney Walsh. Hearing only the rattle of the stumps behind him but not umpire Clyde Duncan's no-ball call, he headed for the pavilion in the direction of extra cover in the mistaken belief that he was out.

Watching Jones leave the crease, Carl Hooper rushed in from the slips, picked up the ball and uprooted the middle stump and appealed. Despite his batting partner, Allan Border, trying to warn Jones of the impending danger, he could not get his bat down quick enough and the square-leg umpire, Clyde Cumberbatch, gave him out.

This decision was in contravention of Law 38.2, which says, 'If a no-ball has been called, the striker shall not be given run out unless he attempts to run' which Jones obviously had not. Surprisingly, both the umpires and captains, Allan Border and Viv Richards, did not know about this Law. This was no consolation for Deano.

One wished Richards had shown sportsmanship to recall Jones, as India's captain M.S. Dhoni reinstated England's batsman Ian Bell in the Trent Bridge Test of 2011, which is detailed elsewhere.

There would have been riots on the ground had the same fate befallen a West Indies batsman in the 1991 Guyana Test.

After retirement from cricket, Dean Jones became a television commentator. But when heard calling South Africa's bearded Muslim batsman Hashim Amla a 'terrorist' on live television he was sacked by his employers, Ten Sports, during the 2006 Sri Lanka v. South Africa Colombo Test. When Amla, who is a devout Muslim, took the catch to dismiss Kumar Sangakkara, Jones was heard to say 'the terrorist has got another wicket'. This created anguish among South Africans.

Shortly afterwards, Jones told journalists at the Colombo airport, 'I'm gone, I'm on the 1 a.m. flight,' he admitted:

> It was a silly and completely insensitive thing to say and, obviously, it was never supposed to be heard over the air. I am truly sorry to have caused offence to anybody and the last thing I intended was to be disrespectful. Everyone needs to get away from perpetuating the myth, publicly and privately, that beards associated with the Muslim faith are somehow suspicious, and I intend to do exactly that. The irony is that I am great friends with most of the Pakistan team and they are all Muslims.
>
> I have no end of respect for the Muslim faith—that's why I'm so sorry at making such a stupid comment. It does not represent who I am, how I think or what I believe. I will be the first person to apologise to Hashim as soon as I get the chance, and I will assure him that prejudice against anybody, on any basis, is unacceptable and not something I will ever condone.

Dean Jones was a complex character. Australia's Test great Bob Simpson summed him up as 'frustrating, exciting, reliable, unreliable, selfish, unselfish, a mug lair and a team player'. He added that Jones' unpredictability was an inherent part of his charm.

BRIBERY, MATCH-FIXING
AND OTHER
CORRUPTIONS

No wonder the 1990s were called the naughty nineties. Not that bribery, match-fixing, ball-tampering and drugs were not prevalent in the past, as already narrated in the previous chapters. But they hit the absolute nadir when three high profile cricketers from three countries, and each a Test captain, were caught with their 'pants down'.

South Africa's Hansie Cronje and India's Mohammad Azharuddin were respected figures on the cricket field and highly revered for their batting and integrity. Both were God-fearing individuals. Pakistan's Salim Malik was also a stylish batsman.

But when the news broke about the involvement of Cronje and Azharuddin in match-fixing, I could not believe it. I remember losing my cool at a party when someone mentioned about Cronje throwing matches in receipt of huge cash payments from the bookmakers. 'Don't you believe all you read in media,' I had argued.

But as the Cronje–Azhar affair came out in the open, I had to eat my words. Now who to trust if you can't trust people like them? As Cronje confessed to Dr Ali Bacher, the face and soul of South African cricket in recent decades and also the managing director of South African Cricket, 'I'm sorry Doc.' Cronje continued haltingly over the phone. 'I haven't been honest with you ... In a moment of stupidity and weakness I allowed Satan and the world to dictate terms with me. The moment I took my eye off Jesus my whole world turned dark.'

At first Cronje pleaded his innocence and most believed him. But the tapes released by the Indian Police proved his guilt. It was massive corruption, just not a one-off error of judgement. As a captain of South Africa he had accepted bribes of around US$100 000 for match-fixing on numerous occasions, even implicating members of his team during South Africa's tours of India in 1996 and 2000.

Cronje's double life was discovered by sheer chance through conversations secretly taped by Indian police. 'These tapes had been made by New Delhi police when the South African team was staying at Delhi's Taj Palace Hotel in mid-March 2000,' wrote Ken Piesse in *Cricket's Greatest Scandals* (2001). 'The damning conversations between Cronje and a London-based bookmaker and garment manufacturer, Sanjeev (Sanjay) Chawla, were recorded—triggering the biggest hue and cry in South African cricket history.'

It was by sheer chance that Cronje's conversation with bookie Chawla was taped. All the police were interested in at the time was to investigate an extortion link involving Dubai gangsters and Dawood Ibrahim, a notorious Mumbai underworld figure.

The police were only checking lists of regularly dialled international phone numbers at the Hotel. In doing so, they tapped into Room 346 where Cronje was having a surreptitious conversation with Chawla as to who was playing in the next match, how much should he score (under 20 runs?), what the team score should be (at least 250?), how much he will receive if he keeps his side of the bargain ...

When the police realised that the conversation was about cricket of a sensationally controversial nature, they kept listening and taping. What a scoop! This historic taping was done by Ishwar Singh Redhu, Delhi's crime branch

At first Cronje pleaded his innocence and most believed him. But the tapes released by the Indian Police proved his guilt. It was massive corruption, just not a one-off error of judgement. As a captain of South Africa he had accepted bribes of around US$100 000 for match–fixing on numerous occasions, even implicating members of his team during South Africa's tours of India in 1996 and 2000.

detective and his team on 7 April 2000. In London, *The Observer* magazine quoted a South African journalist as saying that the voice on the tape was not Cronje's but had an Indian accent. It so turned out that what he had heard were the voices of Indian actors reading out transcripts released by the Delhi Police. The original tapes were sealed and placed under the jurisdiction of the Delhi High Court.

Thus Cronje was in a corner and had to admit his guilt of accepting bribes of up to US$100 000, smuggling it undeclared into South Africa and hiding much of it around his Bloemfontein home. By associating with the cricket underworld, contriving results and implicating others, he had brought notoriety upon himself, his teammates, his family and on the good name of cricket. The other players he had involved were Herschelle Gibbs, Henry Williams, Nico Boje and Pieter Strydom, although everyone did not cooperate with him.

Cronje had been living a double life for many years until caught in 2000. On accepting his guilt he stated as to how bookmakers had hounded him with almost twenty phone calls a day while he was touring India in 2000. He told the inquiry about his love of money, which bordered on sickness. What was more infuriating was that he was not paid a pittance from his Board, around 1.6 million rand) a year. But, according to him, Satan in the form of temptation and greed was burning within him. He had also contemplated suicide, so ashamed he was.

The 3-week investigation had global effect. Just as bushfires destroy properties in a flash of red and orange, the bribery scandal destroyed careers—both promising and legendary. 'Within two months, all the rumours of match-fixing that had been circulating for years were given substance,' wrote Mihir Bose in *Wisden* 2001.

The story on corruption, bribery and match-fixing on a massive international scale started in 1994, involving Pakistan's captain Salim Malik. After Australia's tour of Pakistan in 1994, Shane Warne, Mark Waugh and Tim May alleged that Malik had offered them bribes to throw matches. During the Karachi Test of September–October 1994, Warne had received a phone call from Pakistan skipper Malik in presence of May. According to Warne he visited Malik's room and Malik offered him US$200 000 for him and May to bowl badly on the final day. Warne refused and told his teammate Tim May, captain Mark Taylor, coach Bob Simpson and manager Col Egar about this offer.

This was the cliffhanging Test, which Pakistan won by one wicket. Needing 314 runs to win, Pakistan was 9 for 258 when no. 11 batsman Mushtaq Ahmed joined Inzamam-ul-Haq. The victory was in Australia's lap but incredibly the last pair added 57 runs to win. For bowling very well in both innings, 3 for 61 and 5 for 89, Warne was adjudged Man of the Match.

'When I went up to the podium to collect my man of the match award Malik brushed past me and said that I should have taken the money,' wrote Warne in *Shane Warne – My Autobiography* (2001). 'I wanted to nail him there and then with the old knuckle sandwich.'

Australia's chief executive Graham Halbish called the allegation of three Australian players who were offered bribes by the Pakistan captain as 'cricket's greatest crisis for 20 years'. Wrote David Hopps in *Wisden* 1996, 'If the Salim Malik Affair is ultimately survived without excessive disorder, it will be largely due to the game's inclination to suppress a scandal rather than investigate it.' The ICC failed to take a central role by conducting an immediate inquiry.

They preferred to act as a conduit between the Pakistani and Australian Cricket Boards. Malik was cleared of the allegation by an independent inquiry in Pakistan. Soon after, the Pakistan Cricket Board placed matters in the hands of Fakhruddin Ebrahim, a former Pakistani Supreme Court judge. However, his investigation was hampered by Australia's unwillingness to subject their three players, Warne, Mark Waugh and May, to cross-examination in Pakistan, fearing for their safety. This hampered proper investigation and Judge Ebrahim concluded on 21 October 1995 that the allegations against Salim Malik were unfounded.

Warne explained in his autobiography, '...it was not unreasonable to be worried for our safety if May, Mark Waugh and I went over to Pakistan to give evidence at the original inquiry. In any case, we had given full statements to the ACB and had nothing to hide'.

After the series and the accusation, Malik (some Australian cricketers nicknamed him 'Salim The Rat') was replaced as captain and suspended, pending investigation. Still three months later he captained Pakistan to South Africa and Zimbabwe. He was retained as a batsman when Pakistan toured Australia in November 1995. Warne had the last laugh when he dismissed him fourth ball in the first Test in Brisbane for a duck. This made Warne, with eleven wickets in the match, wisecrack: 'It shows there is justice in the game.'

After the match-fixing accusations against Salim Malik by the Australians in early 1995, there had been inquiries in India, Pakistan and Sri Lanka, as well as media investigations by Indian magazine *Outlook*.

In 2000, Malik became the first player to be banned from cricket for match-fixing, when Justice Qayyum's inquiry found him guilty. He protested his innocence, appealed against the ban in 2001 but the Lahore High Court rejected it. He sought relief from the Supreme Court and after a 7-year wait, had his ban lifted. The gifted wristy batsman had played 103 Tests and 283 ODIs from 1982 to 1999 but the lure of money destroyed his career.

There is a twist in the tail in this nauseating saga. The accusers Warne and Mark Waugh also had their low moments in 1998 when it emerged that they had accepted money from a bookmaker during a short tour of Sri Lanka for a 4-nation one-day tournament in Colombo in September 1994. John, the Indian bookmaker, had met the two Aussie greats at a casino in Colombo and offered money in exchange for information on pitch and weather conditions. They accepted the money, US$5000 and US$6000, respectively. It must be stated that they did not fix a match nor were they ever suspected of doing so.

In February 1995, the Australian Cricket Board (ACB) secretly fined them A$8000 and A$10 000 respectively for their involvement with the bookmaker. However, apart from imposing fines on them, the ACB and the ICC did nothing. This came out in the open in December 1998 when ACB chief executive Malcolm Speed revealed this to the *Australian* cricket writer Malcolm Conn.

Former ACB chairman said the matter was deliberately kept quiet at the time because it was regarded as an internal disciplinary matter.

In *Mark Waugh – the Biography* (2002), author James Knight wrote that Mark accepted the money but told John, who turned out to be a bookmaker, that he would not under any circumstances talk about team tactics or line–ups. Mark Waugh recalled:

I treat people the way they treat me. In that regard I'm a bit naive. I don't see the bad in people, so obviously when I met John I took him at face value. I thought someone was going to give me a bit of money to give a bit of information on pitch and weather conditions [until the end of Australian 1994–95 home season]. I didn't know it was illegal or against the code of conduct. I thought there was no problem with it, otherwise I wouldn't have done it.

I didn't see it as a deceitful thing. I just saw it at face value–he's going to give me some money to tell him about the pitch and the weather, and the general feeling in the team ... To me it's no different from doing a radio interview before a game. You talk about how you are going, whether the pitch is going to keep low or seam a bit, whether it's good to bat on first. It's the same thing you do in a radio interview—that's how I took it.'

A few days later he introduced John to Shane Warne saying that John is someone who 'bets on cricket'. Both Waugh and Warne knew that John betted on cricket but did not know then that he was a bookmaker. In *Shane Warne – My Autobiography* (2001), Warne wrote, 'He [John] said that he was a very wealthy man and wanted to give me something as his way of saying thanks for the number of times he had won on Australia in the past.'

Warne added that in the casino he had lost about A$5000 on a roulette wheel that night. To his surprise John pulled out an envelope full of money. He said it was a token of his appreciation and compensation for the money Warne had lost on the roulette wheel. At first Warne refused the money but John was persistent and said he would be offended if he did not take it. John stressed that he did not expect anything in return so in the end he took it.

Warne explained that he was never under the impression that he was giving information to a bookmaker. 'I just assumed that he [John] was a mate of Mark [Waugh] who was having a bet on cricket. As captain of Victoria and occasionally Australia I gave more information to media than I gave to "John".'

Later he realised that it was a big mistake. 'If something similar had happened to a player today [in 2001] the bells would ring immediately. But in 1994 none of us imagined how aspects of the game might be corrupt.'

The two legendary but gullible Australians should have said: 'Get lost' but they fell for the trick and regretted it later. It should be mentioned here that the whole squad was warned by their coach Bob Simpson at a team meeting to be on guard against people offering gifts. So was it just naivety?

'We all make mistakes', wrote Warne. 'When the news finally broke four years later people were naturally suspicious that they [ACB] had kept the matter under wraps and that there was more to it. Innocently, the Board made a mistake trying to look after us.'

Without trying to play down the errors of judgement on part of Mark Waugh and Shane Warne, the major controversy revolved round Hansie Cronje and Mohammad Azharuddin at the turn of the millennium. We have discussed at length the Cronje crisis. Now to the sudden rise and instant fall of Azharuddin, the captain of India and a religious man everyone looked up to. He was a polite, quiet and sensitive person.

His Test career had a fairytale beginning, becoming the only cricketer to score a century in his first three Tests (against England in India in 1984–85), and a nightmarish ending. In his 99th and final Test, the 37–year old scored 102 runs in the second innings against South Africa in Bangalore in March 2000. It was a dazzling innings replete with glorious drives and wristy onside strokes as he hit 13 fours and 2 sixes out of India's moderate total of 250.

No one had an inkling then that this would be his swan song. After this series, the Hansie Cronje match-fixing scandal came out in the open and rocked the cricket world. During investigations in South Africa, Cronje stated that Azhar (short for Azharuddin) had introduced him to a bookmaker who had offered him the bribe. Azhar denied the allegation strongly but later admitted to certain acts of indiscretion. He was banned from playing any form of cricket. What a way to go after scoring 6215 runs at 45.03 with 22 centuries in 99 Tests, playing 334 ODIs and captaining India in three World Cups during a 16-year international career.

Azhar, then 38, was handed a life ban by the BCCI in December 2000 following the match-fixing inquiry by India's Central Bureau of Investigation (CBI). He plummeted in disgrace when details of his dalliances with bookmakers were made public.

Azhar, then 38, was handed a life ban by the BCCI in December 2000 following the match-fixing inquiry by India's Central Bureau of Investigation (CBI). He plummeted in disgrace when details of his dalliances with bookmakers were made public.

K. Madhavan led the inquiry and concluded that he was guilty of match-fixing with three other Indian Test cricketers Manoj Prabhakar, Ajay Jadeja and Ajay Sharma. It was alleged that Azhar accepted large sums of money from bookmaker Mukesh Kumar Gupta. It was reported that Azhar had later admitted to 'doing' 3 one-day internationals between 1996 and 1999.

All three protested their innocence with Azhar claiming that the CBI was not interested in his side of the story. Apart from the life ban on Azhar and Sharma, Jadeja and Prabhakar were suspended from the game for five years.

Board president A.C. Muthiah after a meeting of the Board's disciplinary committee meeting in Chennai, said:

These hard decisions have been taken after careful consideration. They will set an example for the future. This is a sad day in the annals of Indian cricket. There is clear evidence of match-fixing against Azharuddin. There is also evidence that Sharma acted as a conduit for match-fixing. That's why we clubbed the two of them together and gave life bans. Others had a nexus with bookmakers and introduced players to the bookmakers which is a serious breach of cricketing codes.

Before the CBI report became public, Azharuddin had said that he was being targeted, because as a Muslim, he belonged to a minority community. This was absurd as there was no religion bias when he was appointed as India's captain in 47 Tests (the record he shares with Sunil Gavaskar) and in three World Cups.

Azharuddin later admitted on further questioning that he was first introduced to M.K. Gupta by Ajay Sharma sometime in 1995, at Hotel Taj Palace, New Delhi. Ajay Sharma and Gupta had been approaching him to underperform in some matches for a considerable sum of money. Gupta had offered him a sum of Rs. 1.25 crore (approximately A$270,000 and £182,000), but the deal did not materialise. He accepted that he had taken money on some occasions from MK Gupta but did not underperform in most of the matches in which he had taken money. He stated that the Titan Cup match between India and South Africa at Rajkot, India, in 1996 was fixed through Gupta, and revealed that Ajay Jadeja and Nayan Mongia were also involved along with him. A match in Pepsi Asia Cup in Sri Lanka in 1997 was also fixed through Gupta. Azhar accepted that he had introduced M.K. Gupta to Hansie Cronje at Kanpur in 1996.

By the mid–1990s, Azharuddin was a millionaire in Western terms. Gupta claimed to have initially paid him 90 lakh rupees (A$400 000). Ken Piesse wrote in *Cricket's Greatest Scandals*:

These hard decisions have been taken after careful consideration. They will set an example for the future. This is a sad day in the annals of Indian cricket. There is clear evidence of match–fixing against Azharuddin. There is also evidence that Sharma acted as a conduit for match–fixing.

In July 2000, amid reports of Azharuddin having accumulated wealth and property beyond the horizons of anyone bar Indian royalty and the megastars of business, tax investigators simultaneously raided his homes in Hyderabad and Mumbai, unearthing an unaccounted A$1.54 million in cash, jewellery, property investments and deposits.

While he still protests his innocence, in most people's eyes Azharuddin committed the gravest crime of all, far worse than swallowing a diuretic or injecting a steroid. He was seen to have betrayed the fans who were so outraged they burnt his effigies. He appealed against the life ban in the courts but the verdict is still awaited. He made his debut as a politician by joining the Congress party in 2009.

Pradeep Magazine commented in *India Today* in December 2000:

The most bizarre and mysterious role in the matter is that of Prabhakar. The scandal began in India in 1997 when Prabhakar wrote, in a signed article in a Delhi-based publication, that he was offered 2.5 million rupees (A$53 000) by a teammate to underperform in a match against Pakistan in 1994. When Prabhakar later said that the player was Kapil Dev, the great Indian all-rounder and team captain, he sent the nation in a tailspin.

This led to a CBI probe that exonerated Kapil but alleged that Prabhakar had played a leading role in introducing international cricketers to Gupta. The names appear as something out of a Who's Who of Cricketing Greats. However, none of these allegations were proved.

The Pakistan Board also took hard decisions. The *Qayyum* Report published in early 2000 called for life bans on Test players Salim Malik and Ata-ur-Rehman.

This murky chapter has a tragic ending. Hansie Cronje died on 1 June 2002, when the cargo plane in which he was travelling crashed on Cradock Peak in the Outeniqua mountain range on its approach to his hometown, George, in the Western Cape. He was only 32 years of age.

Wisden 2003 paid him this tribute:

That fateful weekend, he had hitched a ride with the two pilots of an Air Quarius Hawker Siddeley turboprop after his scheduled flight had been grounded by a hailstorm—a risk-taker to the end. More than a thousand mourners filled the Grey College Chapel for Cronje's funeral, while a thousand more outside watched the service, which was televised nationally, on large screens. It was reported that members of the UCBSA, critical earlier of their captain's betrayal, had been told they would not be welcome, but Bertha Cronje, Hansie's widow, said he would not have agreed with such a ban. The divisions were forgotten as South Africa, a nation rebuilding on forgiveness and reconciliation, mourned, in Gary Kirsten's words, 'a great cricketer, a great performer and a great on-field leader of his country'. It was elsewhere that cricket would still consider Hansie Cronje a tarnished hero.

A BIOGRAPHICAL FILM ON CRONJE WAS released in India in May 2012. His brother Franze Cronje told Indian sports writer Bipin Dani:

We finally have a release of the Hansie movie in India. It has now been 10 years since Hansie's death on 1 June 2002. I produced a feature film and a 5-hour documentary about Hansie in 2008 and we have finally been able to release this movie and the documentary on DVD in India through one of the leading Indian newspapers.

The movie does not attempt to vindicate Hansie in any way. He admitted that he was wrong and the movie shows this clearly. Instead we took great care to portray an honest story, based on Hansie's confessions and interviews with 30 plus friends, family and team members. We even interviewed some bookies. This forms part of the documentary on the Bonus DVD (in total more than 5 hours of footage).

The movie is a full feature film, shot in three continents and eight cities, including Mumbai. Frank Rautenbach plays the part of Hansie in the film.

[24]
THE PORT
ELIZABETH TEST
FRACAS

The November 2001 Test between South Africa and India at Port Elizabeth made history of the wrong type. So dissatisfied was the management of the Indian cricket team and its Board with match referee Mike Denness, a former England Test cricketer, that they refused to play the next Test at Centurion if Denness was not replaced as the referee.

When the ICC rejected India's demand, the Indian Board threatened to abort the tour. Financial losses and government pressure were behind the South African Cricket Board to agree to go ahead with an unofficial test with South Africa's former Test wicketkeeper Denis Lindsay as the match referee.

Dicky Rutnagur wrote in *Wisden* 2003, 'The tourists were mere bystanders while war was waged on their behalf by Jagmohan Dalmiya, newly elected President of the Indian Board and also a former President of the ICC.' Dalmiya also demanded a review of the penalties imposed by Denness on six Indian cricketers.

The Port Elizabeth Test was the second in the series with South Africa leading 1–0. Sourav Ganguly won the toss and opted to field. With opening batsman Herschelle Gibbs scoring 196, the home team made 362. India trailed by 161 runs but hit back as South Africa lost 3 for 26, 4 for 91 and 5 for 139 in the second innings. During a valuable partnership between Jacques Kallis and captain Shaun Pollock on a rain-interrupted day, Indian fielders Harbhajan Singh, Virender Sehwag, Shiv Sunder Das and wicketkeeper Deep Dasgupta had allegedly violated the Code of Conduct by charging at the umpire, according to the match referee Denness.

'The tourists were mere bystanders while war was waged on their behalf by Jagmohan Dalmiya, newly elected President of the Indian Board and also a former president of the ICC.' Dalmiya also demanded a review of the penalties imposed by Denness on six Indian cricketers.

More serious was the allegation by him that Sachin Tendulkar had also brought the game into disrepute through 'interference with the match ball, thus changing its condition'. This statement implied that Tendulkar had tampered with the ball and was a cheat. At first, Denness refused to comment on his verdicts or penalties, but he later issued a vague explanation on the Tendulkar case. It suggested that Tendulkar had not tampered with the ball, but had failed to observe the technicality of asking the umpires to supervise removal of mud from the seam of the ball.

Denness added that there had been no complaint from the umpires but he had acted on his own initiative after seeing the video footage. Tendulkar, who had an unblemished record, was fined 75 per cent of his match fee, with a suspended ban for one Test. The Indian public was outraged at the slight against their idol's character. There were street 'morchas' (protest marches) throughout India and scenes of uproar even in the Parliament.

What angered the Indians more was that Denness had overlooked a highly aggressive appeal by Pollock when the tourists were batting. This reinforced the general belief held in the Indian subcontinent that some ICC match referees are racially biased.

To quote respected cricket commentator Harsha Bhogle from *Wisden Cricket Monthly* (January 2002):

Put Virender Sehwag's appeals alongside two of Shaun Pollock's appeals, watch the TV evidence and I challenge anybody, absolutely anybody, to say that one was more intimidatory than the other. One of Pollock's two lbw appeals was made despite one of the biggest inside edges you will ever see. India had reason to be angry.

Apart from the penalties to the five Indian players mentioned above, skipper Sourav Ganguly also received a suspended ban for not upholding the spirit of the game and failing to control his players' on-field conduct.

Of the six Indians who allegedly breached the Code of Conduct, Sehwag was the most severely penalised because he was deemed to have committed two offences. In common with bowler Harbhajan, wicketkeeper Dasgupta, and fielder Das, Sehwag was found guilty of expressing dissent and attempting to intimidate the umpire by charging at him. Sehwag's other offence was the use of 'crude or abusive language'.

'Then came the Tendulkar issue,' wrote Bhogle:

By Denness's own admission he was not tampering with the ball, nor even picking the seam. He was merely taking the grass off the seam—an offence but a minor one. The punishment was extraordinary, not so much because of the fine and suspended sentence, but because of the opportunity it gave the world to call an honest man a cheat ... You don't handcuff an honourable man and put him in jail because he stopped his car six inches beyond the red light.

Also, Denness had passed on the judgement off his own bat and without any complaints from the on-field umpires.

It may be recalled that in the Lord's Test against South Africa in July 1994, match referee Peter Burge from Australia had trusted England's Test captain Michael Atherton till the 'dirt in the pocket' incident was proved as illegal later on.

Besides being suspended for one Test, Sehwag—like the five reported players—was fined 75 per cent of his match fee. The Test left a bitter taste in the mouth. It also led to the ICC planning to reform the referee system.

HAIR, INZY AND
THE FORFEITED
OVAL TEST

W here umpire Darrell Hair is, can controversies be far behind? Let me rephrase that. Where controversy is, can Hair be far behind–either at the bowler's end or at square–leg, or writing hard–hitting books? His no–balling Muttiah Muralitharan for chucking in the 1995 Boxing Day Test in Melbourne has been detailed in the chapter 20.

Although the tall, no–nonsense Australian umpire Hair hates to be called controversial, many describe him as the 'Daddy' of them all. There are no sides to him. What you see is what you get. To be popular is very low on his agenda. Well, popularity is not on his agenda at all. He appears self–righteous and obstinate. But as a person he is friendly and plays guitar in his retirement as he did in his youth, being then a fan of Pink Floyd, the English rock band.

But was he too pedantic? Stephen Fay wrote in *Wisden* 2007:

During England's tour of Pakistan in late 2005, Hair's manner was thought overbearing, and some of his decisions dubious. The reservations went beyond Asia... In 2004, MCC chose him as a consultant on the Laws of Cricket, and in this role he appeared more committed to the strict application of the law than its spirit.

According to Hair, he is the only person to fight against the way cricket administrators are getting soft, which is not in the best interest of the game. That is exactly the title of his second book, *In the Best Interests of the Game* (2011). In it he goes into detail about the reasons why he and fellow umpire Billy Doctrove awarded the 2006 Oval Test to England against Pakistan. This was the first ever forfeit in 1814 Tests spanning 129 years.

The 20 August 2006 is a day to forget for cricket–lovers, as it is the day that cricket plunged into a crisis. It was the fourth day of the fourth and final Test of the series with England leading 2–0. But Pakistan held the upper hand throughout this Test. They bowled out England for 173 and scored 504 to lead by 331 runs, the bearded Mohammad Yusuf topscoring with 128. England was struggling at 4 for 298–still 33 runs in deficit–when it happened.

The first sign of the crisis was at 2.30 p.m. on the fourth day when the fourth umpire Trevor Jesty brought out a box of balls. As the ball was 56-overs old it was presumed it had gone out of shape due to wear and tear. As Hugh Chevallier wrote in *Wisden* 2007, 'However the choice of its replacement fell not to the umpires, but *to the batsmen*—an indication that the officials believed that the ball had been doctored.'

Five minutes later, the umpires removed the bails and returned to the pavilion followed by Collingwood and Bell. The spectators were at a loss as to what was happening. So were the commentators and everyone in the press box.

Umpire Hair then tapped his left shoulder with his right hand and five penalty runs were awarded to England's total. There was confusion all round. What was happening? If the umpire(s) thought the ball was doctored, they apparently did not ask the Pakistanis any questions or give them any warning or any opportunity to defend themselves. It was all based on suspicion and not on thorough investigation and cross–examination. The tourists were publicly found guilty of tampering with the ball on visual observation of the ball's condition but without any proof. Despite the 26 TV cameras scanning the field of play, no one was seen altering the condition of the ball.

Pakistan captain Inzamam–ul–Haq was too stunned to take any action. The Test continued until bad light stopped play at 3.47 p.m. It was the 72nd over of the innings, seventeen overs after the ball was changed. With the light improving, the umpires set out for the Test to continue at 4.55 p.m. Unbeaten batsmen Paul Collingwood and Ian Bell were ready to step out and were seen on the balcony but there was no sign of the Pakistani team.

Five minutes later, the umpires removed the bails and returned to the pavilion followed by Collingwood and Bell. The spectators were at a loss as to what was happening. So were the commentators and everyone in the press box.

The door of the dressing room of the visitors remained shut as the ball–changing incident was hotly discussed. The debate went on at a diplomatic level with English Cricket Board chairman David Morgan and the Pakistan Cricket Board chief Shaharyat Khan discussing the pros and cons. The Pakistani team was livid at being accused of ball tampering without evidence and warning. However, they were persuaded to abandon their protest and Inzamam led his team to the field at 5.23 p.m.—28 minutes after the umpires had.

By then the umpires had returned to the pavilion. What a tableaux; first there were umpires and no fielders and then fielders but no umpires. The baffled spectators, 23 000 of them, booed and jeered as the announcement came that play was called off for the day. Four hours later it was confirmed that the match was over and England had won. For not coming on the field for 28 minutes, the umpires had considered this as a forfeit by the Pakistanis.

Then all hell broke out, newspapers were putting cricket on the front pages with screaming headlines.

Both the parties were in the wrong. Inzamam should have protested on the field when the ball was changed and penalty runs awarded to England, asking for the reasons behind this action. When the Pakistan team did not take the field, Hair and Doctrove waited for five minutes and visited the Pakistani dressing room.

As reported in *In the Best Interests of the Game*, Hair asked Inzamam as to why he did not take the field after the tea interval. Inzamam answered the question with a question: 'Why did you change the ball, there was nothing wrong with it.' Hair replied, 'That is a matter for another time and place. At the moment we need to know if you intend to resume play ... Can you please tell us now if you intend to take the field and if you do not follow us, the match will be considered forfeited by Pakistan and will be awarded to England.'

The door of the dressing room of the visitors remained shut as the ball–changing incident was hotly discussed. The debate went on at a diplomatic level with English Cricket Board chairman David Morgan and the Pakistan Cricket Board chief Shaharyat Khan discussing the pros and cons.

When the Pakistani team did not take the field, Hair informed match referee Mike Procter that Pakistan had forfeited and the match must be awarded to England. The former English umpire, David Shepherd (who had umpired 92 Tests and 172 ODIs), later commented:

The greater crime was not the ball–tampering but the fact that the match ended: the game is sacrosanct. I'm not sure how much dialogue there was between the umpires and Inzamam: it was unfortunate Darrell did not have a more senior partner because Billy [Doctrove] just seemed to go along with it ... There's room for a quiet word, an unofficial warning, if an umpire suspects something. That's what I'd have done.

The English and Pakistani Boards, both the teams and referee Mike Procter had wanted the match to resume the next morning, the fifth day of the Test, but the umpires refused point blank. England won the Test despite being 331 runs in arrears in the first innings and being four down for 298 in the second innings.

The English and Pakistani Boards, both the teams and referee Mike Procter had wanted the match to resume the next morning, the fifth day of the Test, but the umpires refused point blank. England won the Test despite being 331 runs in arrears in the first innings and being four down for 298 in the second innings. As Maxwell Smart in the TV sitcom *Get Smart* would exclaim in his nasal tone: 'Would you believe it?' However, this was not a TV sitcom, it was a 'crigedy' (short for cricket tragedy) with cricket being the loser.

Now to Darrell Hair's version of the dramatic turn of events from his autobiography *In the Best Interests of the Game*. He had inspected the ball after over number 51 and found it satisfactory:

> The next four overs produced just 11 runs. [Kevin] Pietersen struck a boundary through the covers off Danish Kaneria, the ball just reaching the boundary rope at deep cover.
>
> At the end of over 55, I inspected the ball again and was immediately horrified by what I saw. Deep, crescent-shaped scratches had appeared along one quarter section of the ball. In addition, several crescent-shaped indentations were clearly evident on another section of the ball. Both of these areas of scratching and indentations had appeared on the same side of the ball.
>
> It looked as though the ball had been attacked with a blunt knife or similar object. Although I don't believe for a moment that any of the Pakistan team were carrying such an implement, the condition of the ball had definitely changed considerably in a short period of time, and such deterioration was not consistent with the way the game had progressed since Alistair Cook's dismissal [four overs earlier].

Hair explained that there were only five scoring shots in those four overs and of those there was only one forceful stroke—the boundary by Pietersen. Hair was certain that someone had interfered with the surface of the ball. It could not have been caused by the ball hitting the boundary boards, as the Pakistanis had claimed.

He consulted Doctrove and showed him the ball and according to Hair, Doctrove was also horrified. According to Hair, that left the umpires with two alternatives: either ignore the incident or change the ball as required under the Laws of Cricket. They followed the letter of the law.

Hair continued, 'Inzamam was later to repeat on many occasions that he was not told why the ball had been changed. He was. During that prolonged discussion on the field we certainly were not talking about what was the menu for dinner or who would have won the 2.50 at Ascot!'

The biggest shock of it all came five days later, on 25 August 2006. The ICC chief executive flew to London to release e-mails from Hair who had offered to resign from the elite panel of umpires in return for US$500 000. This is an abstract from the e-mail Hair had sent to Doug Cowie, ICC's Manager for Umpires, on 22 August 2006, as reprinted from *In the Best Interests of the Game*:

I am prepared to retire / stand down / relinquish my position on the elite panel to take effect from 31st August 2006 on the following terms: A one-off payment to compensate the loss of future earnings and retainer payment over the next four years which I believe would have been the best years I have to offer ICC and world umpiring. This payment is to be the sum of US$500 000–details of which must be kept confidential by both parties. This sum to be paid directly into my account by 31st August 2006.
ICC may announce the retirement in any way they wish, but I would prefer a simple 'lifestyle choice' as this was the very reason I moved from Australia to settle in the UK three years ago.'

When this e-mail was made public, Hair came in for a lot of criticism. As a result of this furore, he spent two years in international wilderness and was suspended by the ICC before returning to the ICC's elite panel for two Test matches during New Zealand's tour of England in 2008. He then stepped down from the ICC elite panel of umpires to become the CEO of the New South Wales Cricket Umpires and Scorers Association.

'They tried to destroy my life,' he told the *Daily Telegraph*. 'After the ICC made the decision several ICC officials set out to make a real meal of it and make life very tough for me. People like myself pay for standing up for what is right.'

Meanwhile what about the status of The Oval 2006 Test? In 2008, the ICC changed the result of the forfeited Test from an England win to a draw, in contravention of the Laws of cricket, only to rescind their decision in January 2009.

Earlier in October 2007, Hair had sued the ICC for racial discrimination, based on the fact that only he was punished and not Billy Doctrove, his colleague in the 2006 Oval Test. But he withdrew the charges after seven days. In March 2008, he was reinstated by the ICC after a 6-month rehabilitation period, having not been officially removed from the Elite panel of umpires, officiating in two Tests between England and New Zealand in England.

The Nottingham Test of June 2008 proved to be his swan song and he resigned after 17 years of top-level umpiring to concentrate on development and coaching. He had umpired in 44 Tests (then a record for an Australian) and in 75 one-day internationals. He will be remembered by posterity for his controversial decisions in two Tests, the 1995 Boxing Day Test and The Oval Test of 2006.

He was a no-nonsense self-righteous person who called a spade a spade, even when the spade fell on his own toes.

BOB WOOLMER, THE COACH OF PAKISTAN on the 2006 tour to England, hotly denied any ball-tampering by his team but subsequently opined that he believed that ball-tampering should be allowed in cricket and that a modification to existing laws should be made.

GREG CHAPPELL
AND THE
INDIAN
DISCONNECTION

Formerly, it was Australia against England ,for cricket supremacy, which was enlivened with conflicts aplenty. Then it was Australia against New Zealand for their neighbourly pow–wows, not always friendly. Now it is Australia against India for various reasons—tough contests and controversies galore. India's captain Sunil Gavaskar asking his batting partner Chetan Chauhan to walk off the field in the notorious Melbourne Test of 1981 has been described earlier, and the 'Bollyline' hullabaloo between Harbhajan Singh and Andrew Symonds will be described later on in the book.

Less intense but more prolonged was the misunderstanding between India's newly appointed coach Greg Chappell, one of the all-time greatest batsmen, and India's captain and left–hand batsman Sourav Ganguly

Chappell's incisive and no–holds–barred book *Fierce Focus* (2011) gives us an insight into his role as the coach of the Indian cricket team from 2005 to 2007—especially the acrimony with Sourav Ganguly. This assignment, as it turned out, had more thorns than bouquets.

Chappell wrote:

The story really started and finished with Sourav. He played a big part in me getting the job [as coach of India in 2005] and probably expected me to be his saviour, by helping with his batting and supporting the continuation of his captaincy. But we were always working at cross purposes. His idea was probably 'You scratch my back, I'll scratch yours'. He expected I would be so grateful to him for getting me the job that I'd become his henchman in his battle to remain captain. I, on the other hand, took on a job with a primary responsibility to Indian cricket and the Indian people. There were a billion of them and only one Sourav. I wanted to help India become the best cricket team in the world.

But often, best intentions are misunderstood in view of certain Indian cricketers' rock star images. In his home city of Kolkata, Sourav Ganguly was revered as a prince, a Maharaja. But his form was slipping in 2005 as he had reached 33 years of age when Chappell took over as coach.

Chappell believed that if India wanted to become champions in the World Cup or get to the top of Test ranking without Sourav, then so be it. 'From this perspective, I suppose he and I were always on collision course.'

According to Chappell, the Indian media was often at his hotel looking for breaking news stories they could turn into headlines. Many Indians thought that he was a Messiah who would turn India into a winning team in a short time, a tall order. The expectation was just too high and the commitment of some senior players below par. He felt that Ganguly tended to be selfish and self-centred but had praise for Rahul Dravid, Anil Kumble and Sachin Tendulkar. Greg's first assignment was the tour to Sri Lanka. He is critical of the attitude of some Indian players in general. 'Once they were in the Indian cricket team, that was enough, and their motivation was to hold their ground,' Chappell felt. 'I wanted nothing but to help them achieve the careers their rich talent promised.'

Chappell's incisive and no-holds-barred book Fierce Focus (2011) gives us an insight into his role as the coach of the Indian cricket team from 2005 to 2007— especially the acrimony with Sourav Ganguly. This assignment, as it turned out, had more thorns than bouquets.

There is basically a difference between the psyche of Indians and Australian cricketers; the latter basically have that win–win–win attitude, playing hard and giving 100 per cent every time. With exceptions, the Indian cricketers are less determined in their commitment, taking net practice as a chore with that 'whatever will be, will be' attitude. This may be gross generalisation but that is what Chappell felt. He wanted to change this deficiency in a hurry, perhaps too soon for many senior Indian cricketers' liking.

In the words of Darshak Mehta, a business man who knows both Indian and Australian cricket and cricketers:

He [Greg Chappell] articulated great ideas and tackled his job with zeal and skill, with the aim of preparing Indian cricket for a life without its proven superstars. Modernising Indian cricket so quickly was too much for one man to accomplish and there was insufficient leadership to support him.

Mehta opined that his critics did not understand what he was attempting to do, nor realised the considerable resistance he encountered for the change in attitude he wanted.

This must have been music to Greg's ears for he had tried hard to improve Indian cricket but was unappreciated and misunderstood by the hierarchy. The reason he wanted Sourav Ganguly to stand down as captain was because he felt that leadership was affecting his batting.

Few appreciated Greg's ability to pick up talented youngsters from villages and convert them into Test cricketers. Suresh Raina, now an established left-handed Test batsman, told News 24 in an interview that Greg did a great service to Indian cricket as far as promoting youngsters like himself, M.S. Dhoni, Irfan Pathan, S Sreesanth, Murali Karthik, Wasim Jaffer, Piyush Chawla and R.P. Singh, among others. He declared, 'Greg Chappell has always ensured that youngsters get their due in the Indian team.' This must have been music to Greg's ears for he had tried hard to improve Indian cricket but was unappreciated and misunderstood by the hierarchy. The reason he wanted Sourav Ganguly to stand down as captain was because he felt that leadership was affecting his batting. 'I felt strongly that if he gave up the captaincy, he could find a way to batting greatness.' But Sourav wanted to hang on to his leadership. Greg explained:

I did not drop him. He was dropped by the selection panel, of which I was not a member. The chairman, Kiran More, and the other selectors thought that it was time for Sourav to move on and for Rahul to be installed as Captain. I was rather unfairly perceived as the villain—even though anyone who knew what was going on was aware that this move was in the best interest of the team. The story is much greater than me versus Sourav. It was a symptom of a bigger problem of selection having to be form and merit-based, if the team was to achieve its potential.

When Rahul Dravid was handed over the captaincy, Sourav was very much disappointed. He was not the only cricketer Greg did not see eye to eye with. He was disappointed with Virender Sehwag's reluctance to do fielding practice and his reluctance to bat at number four in one-dayers, as Greg had suggested. In retrospect, Sehwag proved his ability to open the innings, being the outstanding success of the 2011 World Cup, which India won at home under Gary Kirsten as the coach.

But this is going ahead of the story. Under Greg, India's performance at both Test and ODI levels improved to a degree. Prior to the 2007 World Cup in the Caribbean, India won the series against the West Indies and Sri Lanka and there was optimism of making it at least to the semi-final of the World Cup. But they were hopelessly eliminated, failing to reach even the Super-8 stage. The star-studded Indians played without spirit and lost to minnows Bangladesh and then to Sri Lanka.

This was a huge disappointment for a billion Indian fans and the effigies of many cricketers were burnt. The media also blamed Greg Chappell for this debacle. It was so heartbreaking for him and his wife Judy who was with him in India during his tenure as India's coach.

This was a huge disappointment for a billion Indian fans and the effigies of many cricketers were burnt. The media also blamed Greg Chappell for this debacle. It was so heartbreaking for him and his wife Judy who was with him in India during his tenure as India's coach. Greg recalled:

> Back in Mumbai, Judy and I were basically under armed guard. There were threats on our lives. Some key people in the BCCI (Board of Control for Cricket in India) were keen for me to continue as coach, but I couldn't see enough signs of commitment to making India the best team in the world.

Also, his doctor had informed him that his blood pressure was high and was surprised how something had not burst. Greg thought of Bob Woolmer, the coach of Pakistan, who was mysteriously found dead in his hotel room in Jamaica during the 2007 World Cup. After much deliberation Greg decided to quit his job, thinking to improve Indian cricket was a 'mission impossible'.

In frank soul-searching, Greg recognised some of his mistakes and wrote in *Fierce Focus*:

I didn't communicate my plans well enough to the senior players. I should have let guys like Tendulkar, Laxman and Sehwag know that although I was an agent of change, they were still part of our [India's] Test cricket future. When I did communicate with them, I was sometimes too abrupt ... My impatience to see improvement across the board was my undoing in the end.

I am an admirer of Greg as a cricketer and a coach, but felt that he lacked tact. Plain talk is well understood in Australia. Not so in India where top cricketers are worshipped and tend to have egos. A car needs both petrol and oil to run smoothly. Greg provided petrol but forgot to top up the oil tank.

There was Chappell's Way–all out determination to succeed with fierce focus as if there was no tomorrow, and the Indian Way–'we'll do net practice tomorrow; too tired now'. But like that 1960s Perry Como song, 'Let's forget about *domani* (tomorrow), for *domani* never comes,' tomorrow never dawns if you don't work at it today. Sadly, the twain of Chappell's Way and India's Way never met, leading to the former's Indian disconnection.

GREG CHAPPELL IS KNOWN AND ADMIRED for his elegant on–drives and brilliant fielding in the slips. But he also has a sense of humour directed at himself. At a Primary Club charity function in Sydney in 1990s, he recalled an experience which brought the house down. He was very nervous before giving a talk on a previous occasion but bravely went ahead as the function was to raise money for charity. The talk must have been a success because he received an ovation. Greg was delighted till a person approached him about ten minutes later and after some 'ers' and 'ums' told him that it was the worst talk he had heard. When a disheartened Greg revealed this to the President, he set his mind at ease by saying, 'Don't you worry about him. He has no brains. He does not think for himself but repeats what everyone else is whispering!'

[27]
HEADLINE HUNTERS —
SHANE AND SHOAIB

Shane Warne is recognised as the best leg–spinner of all time. Not one of *the* greatest but the greatest, the Muhammad Ali of cricket. Both are icons of the games they adorned. They are not only admired for their proficiencies in their respective sport but also as characters of their sports. Neither claimed to be perfect outside their field of speciality. Scandals chased Warne as he grew in stature as a cricketer.

I was fortunate to witness Warne making his Test debut in the Sydney Test against India in January 1992. No one then had an inkling that he would become a cricketing legend as he was hit about all over the ground by Indian batsmen Ravi Shastri and teenage wonder Sachin Tendulkar, only to finish with disappointing figures of one for 150.

He was just as ineffective in the next Test in Adelaide where he went wicketless conceding 78 runs. Fortunately, the selectors had faith in the podgy 22-year old and persevered with him. He ended his Test career from where he had started, on the SCG, in the Ashes Test of January 2007. In a 16-year Test span of highs and highs he had captured 708 wickets at 25.41 in 145 Tests. He was the first bowler to capture 700 Test wickets.

But for the wisdom of Australian selectors, Warne could well have become a two–Test wonder, with the unflattering figures of 68–9–228–1 and a bowling average of 228.00 in the Test series against India in 1991–92. His third Test started as miserably as he went wicket–less again after giving away 107 runs in the first innings of the opening Test against Sri Lanka in Colombo in August 1992. His bowling average deteriorated to 335.00! Still, his captain Allan Border had faith in him when he handed the ball to Warne in the second innings.

Border was desperate. Australia had trailed Sri Lanka by 291 runs. The home team needed 181 runs to win the Test and were 2 for 127, only 54 runs needed for a victory with eight wickets in hand. Courageously, Border gambled on the leg–spin of Warne and he responded with a miracle spell of three wickets for no run and incredibly Australia won by 16 runs.

Then it started happening, Warne's climb to the proverbial Mount Everest. In the Boxing Day 1992 Test in Melbourne, he captured 7 for 52 against the West Indies and was adjudged Man of the Match. It was a match–winning performance. As he told Andy Afford in *Inside Cricket* (January 2011), 'It was only then that

I thought I might be able to play at that level. Until that spell I'd done pretty terribly.'

However, he really arrived on the big scene in the Manchester Test against England in June 1993, his 12th Test. His first ball in an Ashes Test was an unplayable leg-break, which pitched outside Mike Gatting's legs and hit the top of his off stump. So much spin was imparted on the ball that those close to the pitch could hear the buzz in the air. Gatting looked back at the fallen stump in disbelief.

I was fortunate to witness Warne making his Test debut in the Sydney Test against India in January 1992. No one then had an inkling that he would become a cricketing legend as he was hit about all over the ground by Indian batsmen Ravi Shastri and teenage wonder Sachin Tendulkar, only to finish with disappointing figures.

Subsequently, this delivery was dubbed 'the ball of the century' and even more dramatically as 'the ball from hell' and 'the Sultan's Cobra'. Warne had arrived in a big way and was to become a legend as big as Sir Donald Bradman.

Warne is remembered as much for his splendid statistics as for the controversies he was involved in and the headlines he inspired; the ball from hell being the most sensational. He has been named in many controversies, including sex scandals galore—his fingers doing a lot of texting to female admirers, which ultimately finished his marriage to Simone, his involvement with a bookmaker in 1994 (perhaps naively, as described in chapter 23) and drug-taking.

With Man of the Match performances in the semi-final and final, Warne was Australia's star of the 1999 World Cup in England. Four years later he stole the show again but in a negative sort of way. On the eve of their opening fixture against Pakistan at Johannesburg in the 2003 World Cup, a statement from the ACB stated that Warne had failed a routine drugs test and would be heading home to Melbourne immediately. Traces of a banned diuretic—a substance that promotes weight loss but can also be used as a masking agent for steroids—were found in his system. After that Warne produced one of the great excuses in sporting history. He claimed his mother had given him the pill so that he could lose his fat and look good in front of the cameras. That did not convince Dick Pound, the head of the World Anti-Doping Agency.

After this he came back in international cricket performing at his best till retiring after the 2007 Sydney Ashes Test. To his delight, Australia had regained the Ashes by whitewashing England 5–0. He had created another record, which he himself did not know about. Australia had won 92 of the 145 Tests he had played. The Sydney crowd gave him as well as other same day retiring heroes Glenn McGrath and Justin Langer a lap of honour.

Warne was more than just a 708 Test scalp man. He made leg–spinning exciting once again and gave cricket a sexy image.

So dramatic has been Shane's life story that a play was produced in 2009 titled *Shane Warne the Musical*. He now seems more settled after his engagement with English model and actress Liz Hurley in September 2011.

Now to another headline hunter, Pakistan's terrifyingly fast bowler Shoaib Akhtar, the 100 mph man:

According to Australian opening batsman Justin Langer in *Inside Cricket*, January 2009:

He [Shoaib Akhtar] is definitely ranked No. 1 [in his list of fast bowlers]. Nothing compares to Akhtar. No doubt about that. I just can't imagine that anyone can humanly bowl as quick as he does. And the thing about him, he is fast from his first ball to his last so you always have to be on your guard against him.

Ricky Ponting agreed, 'Shoaib's the fastest I've faced.'

Shoaib reached the magical 160 kmph (100 mph) speed on more than one occasion but it was only recognised officially once, during the 2003 World Cup. But his figures are not spectacular in international matches. In a Test span of eleven years from 1997 to 2007, he took 178 wickets at 25.69 in 46 Tests. Because of injuries and controversies he missed almost half the matches Pakistan played. In 163 ODIs he claimed 247 victims at 24.97.

He had it all—express pace, swing, reverse swing, fire in his belly—but was an underachiever. One of sport's most discussed characters, controversies followed his every step; doubt about his action, ball–tampering charges, beating up his own teammates, long bans, heavy fines, injuries, courtroom battles against the Pakistan Cricket Board (PCB) and worst of all doping charges— being tested positive to nandrolone in November 2006 and receiving a 2–year suspension from the PCB.

A few months later he received a 13-match ban after he attacked his fellow opening bowler Mohammad Asif (who had also tested positive to nandrolone) with a bat. That the two cricketers were still available to play was entirely due to the technicalities of the test they had undergone. It had been carried out internally by the PCB who was not a signatory of the WADA (World Anti-doping Agency) agreement at the time. Consequently, the bans were overturned on a technicality, although both men were conveniently injured before the start of the World Cup in the Caribbean in March 2007.

In his autobiography *Controversially Yours* published in 2011 he admitted to ball-tampering. He angered Indian cricket lovers by writing that Sachin Tendulkar shivered when facing him. In the book, Shoaib admitted that he got his PCB ban reversed by pulling political strings.

Did Shoaib chuck? In his book *Umpire's Story* (2003) New Zealand umpire Steve Dunne wrote:

> I might as well make my position clear about [Shoaib] Akhtar. I don't believe he is a chucker, despite the fact that I, along with fellow umpire Doug [Cowie], signed the report asking for his action to be investigated. I've seen the subsequent report produced by the University of Western Australia and it explains what he does with his arm, and that he doesn't throw.

Dunne also recalled the evening he stood in a one-day international in his home town Dunedin when Shoaib unleashed a torrid display of fast bowling. Dunne, and his fellow umpire Doug Cowie, reported Akhtar to match referee Ranjan Madugalle because they weren't completely satisfied with his action.

There may be doubts about Shoaib's bowling action but there is no doubt about his being frighteningly fast. Two of his best spells came in 2002:

6 for 11 against New Zealand in the first Test at Lahore in May 2002: After Pakistan had amassed 643 (Inzamam-ul-Haq 329), Shoaib got into the act with devastating pace. Of his six victims in the first innings, five were bowled and one declared lbw as his fiery pace and toe-crushing yorkers proved unplayable and the tourists collapsed for 73 and eventually lost by an innings and 324 runs in three days.

5 for 21 against Australia in the first Test at Colombo in October 2002: The

invincible Australians under Steve Waugh totalled 467 and an inexperienced Pakistani team trailed by 188 runs, Shane Warne capturing seven wickets. The Australian openers had added 61 when Shoaib struck. In a dizzy spell he took three prize wickets in four balls. Ponting for 7 and the Waugh twins for ducks. In his next over Shoaib smashed Adam Gilchrist's stumps off a missile from round the wicket before he could complete his stroke. *Wisden* 2004 commented that this was one of Test cricket's greatest short spells. But it was wasted, as Australia won by 41 runs.

The Test was remarkable as spectators saw two of the greatest bowlers at their best, Warne taking 7–94 and 4 for 94 and Shoaib 3 for 51 and 5 for 21.

Apart from his aggro, ego and misdemeanours, Shoaib Akhtar will be remembered for his charismatic personality. I still recall the ecstasy on his face when he bamboozled master batsmen Brian Lara, Ponting or Tendulkar with sheer speed, followed by his imitation of an aeroplane landing. He was a mischievous boy in an adult body.

[28]
BOLLYLINE: THE HARBHAJAN– SYMONDS HULLABALOO

Was it wheels within wheels or was it much–ado about nothing? I refer to the Sydney Test of January 2008. Whereas Bodyline was planned months in advance, 'Bollyline' just happened. Compared to the seriousness of Bodyline (see chapter 6), the Bollyline controversy was trivial, a sort of media-beat up to enliven what appeared a one–sided series. Australia had trounced India by 337 runs in the Boxing Day Melbourne Test less than a week ago and had amassed 463 runs on the second day of the Sydney Test.

To me it was a mini TV series with more villains than heroes, and the blowing up of minor incidents into mega furores with cultural misunderstandings galore. Each day of the 'serial' ended on a high note with a promise of more excitement in the to–be–continued TV soapie the next night, climaxing with the threat of a chartered plane flying the team home unless demands were met.

Greg Baum wrote in *Wisden* 2008, '"Bollyline" in Sydney will go down in history as a kind of cricketing six-day war. It was too real and nasty while it was happening, but it was over almost as soon as it had begun.'

Not so in my opinion. Four years have passed since this controversy as I type this in 2012, and the on–field verbal clashes involving Harbhajan Singh and Andrew Symonds are still discussed hotly. There were more subplots in this drama: the poor umpiring of Steve Bucknor and Mark Benson who made more howlers in one game than others would in a series and Benson's subsequent outing, Australian captain Ricky Ponting's frequent appealing and the noted cricket writer Peter Roebuck calling for his sacking, the Indian captain Anil Kumble saying at the Press Conference at the end of the match that India lost with just nine minutes remaining. The latter declared, 'Only one team was playing in the spirit of the game.'

This was an echo of the Bodyline series when the Australian captain Bill Woodfull had made a similar comment 75 years ago. He had strongly denounced Bodyline as being against the spirit of cricket after being hit on the chest several times. When the MCC Manager Plum Warner went to the Australian Dressing Room in Adelaide, Woodfull had commented, 'There's two teams out there, and only one of them's playing cricket.'

Coming back to the 2008 controversial Sydney Test. Was Harbhajan calling Symonds a 'monkey' or 'teri maki' (a swear word in Hindi language), a racist comment or a sledge? To understand the implication of what is referred to as 'Monkeygate', one has to go back a few months when Australia toured India for a series of 7 one–day internationals. Symonds was the Man of the Series on that tour, scoring most runs (365) and topping the averages (73) with a strike

> *"'Bollyline" in Sydney will go down in history as a kind of cricketing 6-day war. It was too real and nasty while it was happening, but it was over almost as soon as it had begun.'*

rate of 110. 'His fielding was boisterously electric,' wrote Anand Vasu in *Wisden* 2008. Comparisons with master blaster Viv Richards did not appear over the top as Australia triumphed 4–2.

But that series is also remembered for shameful behaviour by sections of the Indian crowds during matches in Vadodra and in Mumbai. The dreadlocked Symonds was subjected to monkey chants from sections of the crowd at these two venues. The villains were caught on camera in Mumbai and thrown out.

Symonds, who had entertained the crowds with his spectacular batting and fielding, must have felt devastated at this shocking treatment. He was the only dark cricketer among white Australians and it appeared racial abuse. If Symonds felt insulted he did not show it till the Sydney Test of January 2008. This is how the drama unfolded.

On the third day of the Test, 4 January 2008, India was replying to Australia's 463, and was seven wickets down for a score of over 400. Harbhajan was engaged in a century partnership with maestro Sachin Tendulkar. In the 116th over, Harbhajan dug out a yorker from fast bowler Brett Lee and took a single.

Adam Gichrist, who was keeping wickets in that Test, wrote in his autobiography *True Colours – My Life* (2008):

They [India] were passing our total, with Harbhajan taking a few lusty swings, when he got one away to fine leg off Brett Lee. As he jogged through for the single Harbhajan gave Brett a light, inoffensive pat on the backside. Brett looked over his shoulder and gave Harbhajan a rueful sort of half smile.

The next thing I saw, Symo [Symonds] had come across the wicket while changing his position and said to Harbhajan something like, 'Don't touch him, you've got no friends out here'. Harbhajan never needed an invitation for a bit of banter, and Symo had given him one. So it was on again, the bickering between the two of them ...

Then at the change of ends, I heard Haydos [Matthew Hayden] and Harbhajan talking to each other. 'You've got a witness now', Haydos was saying.

Gilchrist saw Ponting, Tendulkar and Harbhajan, standing on the wicket, talking. Then he heard Harbhajan say to Ricky, 'Sorry, I apologise, it won't happen again.' Gilchrist added in *True Colours*. 'Both Symo and Haydos had heard him call Symo a monkey.'

Umpire Mark Benson spoke to Harbhajan. The bearded Indian of almost the same skin colour as Symonds continued batting and scored 67 out of India's total of 532.

At stumps, India's skipper Kumble apologised to rival captain Ponting and requested him to talk the matter over and not report it to match referee Mike Procter. Ponting, with his teammates no strangers to sledging, told Kumble that he already had reported the incident to Procter.

The next thing I saw, Symo [Symonds] had come across the wicket while changing his position and said to Harbhajan something like, 'Don't touch him, you've got no friends out here'. Harbhajan never needed an invitation for a bit of banter, and Symo had given him one. So it was on again, the bickering between the two of them ...

That very night at 10.30 p.m. Harbhajan was charged with 'using language or gestures that offend another person on the basis of race, religion, gender, colour, descent or national or ethnic origin'. But there were two versions as to what Harbhajan had told Symonds. The umpires had not heard what was actually said, nor had the stumps–audio recorded what was said. So it was the Australians' word against the Indians' and Procter accepted the Australian version. This angered the Indian cricketers and their followers.

After an over 4-hour hearing on 7 January, a day after the Test concluded, an announcement was made that Harbhajan was given a 3–Test ban. Procter stated, 'I am satisfied beyond a reasonable doubt that Harbhajan Singh directed the word [monkey] at Andrew Symonds and also that he meant it to offend on the basis of Symonds's race or ethnic origin.'

Later he told the *Sydney Morning Herald* that this was not a case of just taking the word of an Australian over that of an Indian.'

What infuriated the Indian team was as to how Procter was 'satisfied beyond a reasonable doubt' that Harbhajan had uttered the word monkey. There was no evidence, video or audio. He had taken the words of the Australians over those of the Indians. India's management called a press conference in the team hotel at 4 a.m. They were highly offended by one particular line in Procter's document: 'I believe that one group was telling the truth.'

Two days later, John Hansen, a New Zealand High Court judge, was appointed appeals commissioner. Both Tendulkar and Harbhajan, the only Indians present on the field during the incident, stated at the appeal that the Australian fielders may have mistaken a derogatory word 'teri maki' uttered by Harbhajan for the disputed word 'monkey'.

The touring team fought fire with fire, complaining to BCCI against umpiring blunders that went mostly against India (Symonds was given three 'lives' by umpires when he was on 30, 48 and 148 and he went on to make 162 not out and eventually adjudged Man of the Match). The visiting team appealed against Harbhajan's ban. They also complained against Australian spinner Brad Hogg calling them 'bastards'. This charge was later dropped.

Two days later, John Hansen, a New Zealand High Court judge, was appointed appeals commissioner. Both Tendulkar and Harbhajan, the only Indians present on the field during the incident, stated at the appeal that the Australian fielders may have mistaken a derogatory word 'teri maki' uttered by Harbhajan for the disputed word 'monkey'.

Judge Hansen decided on 29 January that the charge of racism was not proven. Instead, Harbhajan was found guilty on the lesser offence of 'abuse and insult not amounting to racism' and was fined half his match fee. The very next day Hansen realised a 'database error' by the ICC, who failed to inform him of Harbhajan's earlier disciplinary breaches in November 2001 when given a suspended one–Test ban. Had he known that, Harbhajan would have received a stricter penalty.

The contentious Test series continued with an energised India winning the next Test at Perth, their first-ever victory on this venue, drawing the final Test in Adelaide and winning the tri-nation Commonwealth Bank one-day series, beating Australia in the Final.

Thus ended the controversial series. But just as 'The End' was written at the conclusion of the *Monkeygate* Bollywood movie, Gilchrist wrote a postscript. In his autobiography *True Colours – My Life*, Gilchrist questioned the integrity of leading Indian batsman Tendulkar in relation to the evidence he presented at the hearing. He added that Tendulkar had told at the first investigation that he could not hear what Harbhajan said to Symonds. Gilchrist then questioned why Tendulkar subsequently agreed with Harbhajan's claim at the second hearing that the exchange was an obscenity. He also raised questions over Tendulkar's sportsmanship and said he was 'hard to find for a changing-room handshake after we have beaten India'.

The reaction to this accusation in India was so vehement that it forced Gilchrist to clarify his position. Gilchrist later insisted that he did not accuse Tendulkar of lying in his testimony. He also denied calling the Indian a 'bad sport' in regards to the handshake issue. Tendulkar responded by saying that 'those remarks came from someone who doesn't know me enough. I think he made loose statements ... I reminded him that I was the first person to shake hands after the Sydney defeat.'

This hullabaloo would have been avoided had Ponting accepted Kumble's apology on the third day of the Test and not reported this incident to the match referee. After all, Australian cricketers are not shrinking violets when it comes to sledging their opponents.

On the contrary, some of the Indian cricketers, especially Harbhajan (Bhaji to friends) and Santhakumaran Sreesanth learnt this 'art' from their Australian counterparts, giving back what they have been receiving on a regular basis over the years. True, two wrongs don't make one right, but Ponting getting offended with his new-found holier-than-thou image was like a pot calling a kettle black; oops—not a racist remark!

Just as a telemovie was made of Bodyline, a mini TV series could be made of the Bollyline saga in the future. Will it be a sitcom, a soapie or a Bollywood movie, with dancing on the steps of Brewongle Stand?

THERE HAVE BEEN SEVERAL VERSIONS AS to who coined the word 'Bodyline'. Not so for 'Bollyline'. *Sun–Herald* sports writer Paul Cully from Sydney coined the word. When usually sedate Indian captain Anil Kumble accused Australia of not playing within the spirit of cricket, Cully put the word 'Bollyline' on the front page of the *Herald* sports edition.' Thanks must also go to former Herald cricket writer Alex Brown', Cully said. Bollyline is an adaption of 'Bodyline' of 1932 with 'Bollywood', the multibillion film industry of India, as affluent as Hollywood and twice its size.

There was another postscript to the Harbhajan saga. Three months after the 'monkeygate', Harbhajan slapped teammate Sreesanth after an Indian Premier League Twenty20 match for Mumbai Indians against Kings XI Punjab on 25 April 2008, and was banned from the rest of the IPL season as also for 5 one–day internationals against Bangladesh and Pakistan. For missing out on 11 IPL matches that season he lost around US$730 000. 'What goes around comes around', wrote Adam Gilchrist with smug satisfaction.

Around the time that his bowling action was reported as suspect, Sri Lanka's stylish batsman Kumar Sangakkara sledged Harbhajan: 'Why do you wear short sleeves when batting and long sleeves when bowling?'

Meanwhile, what about Symonds? His off–field attitude continued to be a problem and the last straw came when he went fishing in Darwin when he should have been at a team meeting before an ODI series against Bangladesh in August 2008. He was sent home from the series and not picked for the tour of India later in the year. A breaking of team drinking rules led to his exit from the squad in England on the eve of the 2009 World Twenty20, and his Cricket Australia contract was soon cancelled. Despite his rancour with the Indian team in the Bollyline saga, Symonds was the most popular overseas cricketer at the IPL auction in 2008 where he was auctioned for US$1.3 million, second only to India's M.S. Dhoni. Symonds retired from all cricket in February 2012.

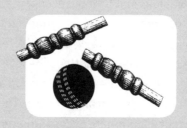

TERRORISM IN
A TEAM BUS

B ut for the presence of mind of bus driver Mehar Mohammad Khalil, it would have been the biggest tragedy in cricket history. But for Khalil putting his foot firmly on the accelerator the whole Sri Lankan cricket team, including skipper Mahela Jayawardene, legendary spinner Muttiah Muralitharan, Kumar Sangakkara and Tillekeratne Dilshan would have perished in a terrorist attack in Lahore. But for ... so many 'but fors'.

This is how the frightening events happened. The series between Pakistan and Sri Lanka had been hastily arranged after India declined to tour Pakistan. Some politicians had accused Pakistan of involvement in the Mumbai terror attacks of November 2008, which killed over 170 people. Earlier, the fear of terrorist attacks and suicide bombers had also caused Australia to abort their tours to Pakistan. But as Sri Lanka had friendly relations with Pakistan, they agreed to tour that country and regretted it.

Some politicians had accused Pakistan of involvement in the Mumbai terror attacks of November 2008, which killed over 170 people. Earlier, the fear of terrorist attacks and suicide bombers had also caused Australia to abort their tours to Pakistan.

The 3 one-day international series went ahead satisfactorily, Pakistan winning the first ODI in Karachi but losing the second in Karachi and the third in Lahore.

The first Test in Karachi was a feast for batsmen, 1553 runs being plundered for only 18 wickets. The visitors started the run-athon by amassing 7 for 644, Mahela Jayawardene 240 and Thilan Samaraweera 231, adding 437 runs for the fourth wicket. Incredibly, Pakistan took a first innings lead of 121 when they declared at 6 for 765, captain Younis Khan hitting 313 and Kamran Akmal an unbeaten 158.

The next Test in Lahore was equally run-rich on the first two days. Sri Lanka declared the innings closed at 7 for 606 with Samaraweera becoming the seventh batsman after Don Bradman (Australia, in 1930, 1934, 1936–37), Wally Hammond (England, 1928–29, 1932–33), Vinod Kambli (India, 1992–93), Graeme Smith (South Africa, 2003), Ricky Ponting (Australia, 2003–04) and Kumar Sangakkara (Sri Lanka, 2007) to hit double centuries in successive Tests.

But the third morning of the Test—3 March 2009—was catastrophic. There was a terrorist attack on the Sri Lankan team bus as it drove to the Lahore Stadium. A dozen gunmen ambushed them at the nearby Liberty Roundabout. Four Sri Lankan players in the bus (including Samaraweera, the double centurion of the previous day) were badly injured but most escaped with minor shrapnel injuries thanks to bus driver Khalil accelerating the bus to reach the safety of the pavilion 500 metres away.

Khalil was feted as a hero and later decorated by the Pakistan Cricket Board, the Pakistan Government and later by the Sri Lankan Government.

Wisden correspondent Qamar Ahmed himself had a narrow escape. As he wrote in *Wisden* 2010, 'If it had not been for my late breakfast, I would have been at the Liberty Roundabout when it happened.'

Others were not so lucky. Six policemen, including a traffic warden and the driver of the umpire's minibus were killed. The fourth umpire, Ahzan Raza, and a liaison officer were badly wounded but survived.

The then ICC President David Morgan said, 'It has completely changed the landscape, not just in the sub-continent. On many occasions we have been told that cricketers would not be targeted in Pakistan. This morning [3 March 2009], events have proved this to be incorrect.'

[30]
IPL SIZZLES
AND FIZZLES

When the Twenty20 Indian Premier League (IPL) was inaugurated in India in 2008 amid fanfare, including scantily-clad cheer girls, it was promoted as 'cricket with more sixes than maidens'. Five years on it has been embroiled in various controversies, including alleged match-fixing, spot-fixing, bribery, booze-soaked parties, sexual charges, assault—climaxed by a mega movie star and owner of a franchise barred from entering Mumbai's Wankhede Stadium.

IPL was the brainchild of Lalit Modi, the first IPL Commissioner. But he was sacked by the BCCI (Board of Control for Cricket in India) in 2010 over 'alleged financial improprieties' and has been living in self-imposed exile in London ever since.

Firstly, here are the the good points of IPL:

- The spectators see the best players from yesterday, today and tomorrow in action.
- Old 'foes' like Harbhajan Singh and Andrew Symonds play side by side for the same team Mumbai Indians, their misunderstandings sorted out.
- Youngsters have a chance to play with and against cricketing legends.
- It provides entertainment for the masses with towering sixes and cliffhanging finishes.

Now the minus point:

Who cares as to who wins? Those cash-laden franchises are neither National nor State teams. They are teams made up of auctioned cricketers who play for money. Bill O'Reilly had described Kerry Packer's World Series Cricket in late 1970s as a circus with clowns (players wearing colour clothing). But in a way most of them were playing for their countries. Worst of all, these get-rich-quick IPL matches have been riddled with malpractices galore. 'Not cricket' just about sums up this mutant sport.

IPL-5, the 2012 edition of IPL, brought out many hidden issues in the open. A secret operation by an Indian TV channel led to the suspension of five cricketers for allegedly accepting bribes. *Hindustan Times*, India, stated that just as spectators and journalists were raving about a number of close and exciting finishes came a TV sting operation that showed that some IPL players were agreeing to spot-fixing, which raised doubts about those last-over finishes being possibly contrived.

On 14 May 2012, an Indian news channel *India TV* aired a sting operation that deceptively caught a person committing some secretive negotiation on television. It caught five players discussing terms and conditions where they would be willing to do spot–fixing. BCCI and the IPL President Rajiv Shukla reacted to the TV news by immediately suspending those five uncapped Indian players: T.P. Sudhindra from the franchise Deccan Chargers, Mohnish Mishra (Pune Warriors), Amit Yadav and Shalabh Srivastava (Kings XI Punjab) as also Abhinav Bali from Delhi.

Mishra admitted to have said that franchises pay black money in a sting operation. He was caught on tape saying that franchises paid them black money and that he had received A$ 300,000 (about £202,000) from the latter, among which A$240,000 (about £162,000) was black money.

Soon after, there was a nasty verbal fight (and fist fight) between India's mega movie star and owner of IPL franchise Kolkata Knight Riders, Shah Rukh Khan, and officials of the Mumbai Cricket Association. He was later banned from entering the Wankhede Stadium, Mumbai. This would be equivalent to Hollywood star Brad Pitt or Nicole Kidman getting banned from an Oscar Night. The reaction was huge in India and some politicians demanded that the IPL, which has been drawing big crowds and TV audiences, be scrapped.

But there is more! An IPL player, Luke Pomersbach from Western Australia and playing for Royal Challengers Bangalore in Delhi, got in deep trouble in the 2012 IPL. No stranger to rowdy behaviour he was suspended for drinking before a crucial match for Western Australia against South Australia in 2007. And in 2009, he was involved in two hit–run incidents when driving a car over the limit.

IPL was the brainchild of Lalit Modi, the first IPL Commissioner. But he was sacked by the BCCI (Board of Control for Cricket in India) in 2010 over 'alleged financial improprieties' and has been living in self–imposed exile in London ever since.

In Delhi in 2012, his cricket career was placed on hold for allegedly molesting an American woman of Indian origin and for assaulting her fiancé in a 5–star hotel. He appeared in a Delhi court where he was granted interim bail. He was also suspended by his IPL franchise for the rest of this tournament.

Sharda Ugra wrote in *Cricinfo*:

The IPL is not the only sports league in the world offering insane salaries and party lifestyles. European football, the NFL and the NBA, to name a few, are full of stories of the kind the IPL has produced this week [May 2012]. These leagues are decades old but the IPL, into its fifth year, is just beginning to identify its conflict zones. It is what happens when money, power, alcohol and entertainment meet entitlement.

Shane Warne had also received a warning for using expletives in IPL-4. His franchise Rajasthan Royals decided to take disciplinary action against him. After an internal probe, his team found the legendary Australian guilty of publicly insulting Sanjay Dixit, the secretary of his franchise. Its CEO, Sean Morris, said, 'The player [Warne] has accepted the action that we have taken and he apologised for any distress caused. We have told all our players that we will not tolerate colourful language towards anyone and in particular not a senior officer.'

There were also scandals involving women that have rocked IPL. The most striking was the role of Sunanda Pushkar, a businesswoman and an Indian celebrity. She was at the centre of a saga that ended with the dismissal of two men from their positions of power. In 2010, then IPL Commissioner Lalit Modi had claimed that Shashi Tharoor, a Cabinet Minister at the time, had gifted Sunanda a stake in Rendezvous Sports World, a co-owner of the Kochi franchise. There were allegations that Pushkar's stake was a proxy for Tharoor.

Modi further alleged that Tharoor had instructed him not to reveal the identities of the stakeholders of the Kochi IPL franchise. Tharoor denied these allegations. The two kept going hammer and tongs at each other. This disharmony was the ideal opportunity for Modi and Tharoor's detractors to unseat both of them.

During IPL-5 in 2012, Preity Zinta, an actress and the co-owner of the Kings XI Punjab franchise, allegedly tangled with umpires over the controversial dismissal of her team's batsman Shaun Marsh. The incident took place in Mohali after Marsh was dismissed in a controversial manner.

He edged a Brett Lee delivery to Kolkata Knight Riders' wicketkeeper Manvinder Bisla, who claimed a clean catch, even though TV replays suggested otherwise. Kings XI Punjab's captain Adam Gilchrist had to apparently calm actress Zinta down after she had rushed onto the ground during the strategic time-out and reportedly clashed with the match officials.

As we go to press, the Mumbai police have reportedly confirmed that Indian leg–spinner Rahul Sharma and the South African fast bowler Wayne Parnell tested positive for recreational drugs. This was after a raid on a party in Mumbai in May 2012. Both had played for Pune Warriors in IPL 2012.

Despite all this 'hoo–ha', IPL will not go away. It is a gloss and glam entertainment wrapped within a business that mints money. The players are tempted because of easy dollars and the crowds lap it up because of the instant gratification.

But is it good for cricket? For example, have a look at what it did to Indian cricketers. They were the lauded and applauded World Cup champions on 2 April 2011. IPL–4 started a week later and the momentum was lost; some got injured and others lost their focus. It would be too simplistic to blame IPL alone for India's pathetic performances in the Test series in England in 2011 and in Australia in 2011–12.

Shane Warne had also received a warning for using expletives in IPL–4. His franchise Rajasthan Royals decided to take disciplinary action against him. After an internal probe, his team found the legendary Australian guilty of publicly insulting Sanjay Dixit, the secretary of his franchise.

Surely there were other reasons but if one does not have fierce focus on the game, the results are disastrous. Quick money–spinners like IPL snap one's concentration, the will to succeed and the determination to win.

There is much more about IPL that needs looking into. It sizzled in its formative years but appears to be fizzling out. The plot thickens.

[31]
DEATH COMES AS THE END —
VALE HOOKES, WOOLMER AND ROEBUCK

S et in Egypt in 2000 BC, *Death Comes as the End* was a best–selling detective novel by Agatha Christie. Shocking deaths of cricketing personalities— David Hookes, Bob Woolmer and Peter Roebuck occurred in 2000 AD–in Melbourne 2004 for Hookes, in Jamaica 2007 for Woolmer and in Cape Town 2011 for Roebuck. All three were colourful multi-talented characters who enriched the game in different ways but the end of the last two remains in a way a mysterious 'who–done–it'.

For handsome Hookes, there was no half way; it was all or nothing. His was a life of contrasts: a sensational start to his Test career and run bonanza in Sheffield Shield, but a shocking end to his life–violently bashed on a street corner outside a pub in Melbourne.

An aggressive left–handed batsman, he made his first–class debut in 1975–76 for South Australia. He was at his prolific best in February 1977 when he scored five centuries from six innings in 17 days. He made 163 and 9, 185 and 105, followed by 135 and 156 in successive innings. He became the first Australian and second in the world after Surrey's Tom Hayward in 1906 to register centuries in each innings of two consecutive first–class matches.

This run–spree led to Hookes's selection in the Centenary Test at the age of 21. Few will forget his eye–catching debut in the above Test in Melbourne the following month when England's captain Tony Greig did not know what hit him.

In front of the largest gathering of international cricketers in history, Hookes smashed Greig for five fours in five balls in an over when scoring 56 in the second innings. Later, Hookes said tongue–in–cheek, 'I made Tony Greig famous.'

However, after such a sensational start Hookes could not maintain his form and was dropped in 1985 with a moderate average of 34.36 in 23 Tests. His only Test century (143 not out) was in Australia's inaugural Test against Sri Lanka at Kandy in April 1983.

It was in first–class cricket that he excelled as he finished his career as the highest run–scorer in Sheffield Shield history. His top score was a chanceless unbeaten 306 for South Australia against Tasmania at Adelaide in March 1987, when he added 462 runs with Wayne Phillips (213 not out) for the unbroken fourth wicket. In this match, skipper Hookes had outscored Tasmania (240 all out and 257 all out) in each innings.

In October 1982, against Victoria, Hookes had slammed a century off 34 balls, belting 17 fours and three sixes. It was the fastest century in Australian domestic cricket. Gideon Haigh referred to him in *The Wisden Cricketer* (March 2004) as 'a first-class destroyer of second-rate bowling'.

Hookes was one of the key figures in World Series Cricket (WSC) and despite a broken jaw from a bouncer from West Indies fast bowler Andy Roberts in a 'Supertest' at the Sydney Showground, he became the third highest scorer for Australia in WSC after Ian and Greg Chappell.

Strong-willed, he had arguments with cricket's administrators. After retiring from cricket in 1992 he became a radio broadcaster and coached Victoria from 2002 onwards with success.

But a tragic end awaited this charismatic player. On the night of 18 January 2004, he went to the Beaconsfield Hotel in Melbourne with members of the Victoria and South Australian teams to celebrate Victoria's win in a one-day ING Cup match. Shortly after midnight, the teams were asked to leave the hotel. It is not clear whether they left the pub voluntarily or were forced to vacate as there are conflicting reports.

The security staff continued following the team members for a short distance outside the hotel and there was an ugly altercation. Eye witnesses gave contradictory testimony of what exactly transpired and who started the fight. But what is not in doubt is that Hookes fell to the ground, hitting his head in the process and he went into cardiac arrest. He was revived by paramedics but did not regain consciousness. He was taken to Melbourne's Alfred Hospital and placed on life support. The following evening, after family and friends had said their goodbyes, Hookes was taken off life support and died shortly afterwards. Hookes, 48, was an organ donor and ten individuals received his transplanted organs.

A memorial service was held on the Adelaide Oval a week later and was attended by his teammates as well as Steve Bracks, the Premier of Victoria. About 10 000 people were present at the service.

The security bouncer at the pub, 22-year-old Zdravko Micevic, who had punched Hookes was charged with manslaughter but was later acquitted. Micevic's lawyer, Terry Forrest, claimed that Hookes had punched his client first without provocation. Forrest also stated that Hookes had a blood-alcohol content of 0.14 at the time of the incident.

But Test batsman Darren Lehmann said at the hearing in November 2004 that despite being in the pub and being close to the group, he had not seen anyone throw 'a violent series of punches' or noticed any boisterous behaviour. According to a report in the *Sydney Morning Herald* of 15 November 2004, Lehmann presented a stoic defence to questioning about his role in the altercation with the bouncers and his observations of the night's events. He repeatedly told the court he either had not seen various incidents described by Mr Forrest or could not recall what was said or done by other members of the group at almost any stage of the night.

End of an innings by David Hookes, *bowled* by a bouncer.

Now to a sensational who–done–it in Jamaica.

Born in Kanpur, India, Bob Woolmer was educated in Kent, England, and played county cricket for Kent as an all–rounder. He made his Test debut for England against Australia in 1975, and in the final Test at The Oval scored a patient 149. All of his 3 Test hundreds were against Australia. His international playing career was stalled when he joined World Series Cricket and ended after joining the rebel tour to South Africa in 1980s.

He then coached Kent, Warwickshire and South Africa before he was appointed coach of Pakistan in 2004. As a coach he was a technophile, always with his laptop equipped with modern coaching methods before they had become popular.

He had reasonable success in Pakistan and had expected a lot from his team for the World Cup in the West Indies. But the unthinkable happened. Although the 2007 World Cup lacked the spectator appeal of the previous Cups, it brought in shocks and traumas as never before. Imagine Pakistan, among two or three nations expected to win the 1991 World Cup, losing to Ireland on St Patrick's Day and crashing out of the World Cup. If this was not enough jolt for the system, Woolmer, 58, was found dead a day after Pakistan's shock loss to Ireland in his Jamaica Pegasus Hotel.

Was his death due to natural causes, did he commit suicide, was he murdered by strangulation or by poison? Let's examine each theory.

Natural cause: A large man, Woolmer had diabetes, an enlarged left ventricle and a distinct narrowing of the coronary arteries. It is known that about 75 per cent of diabetics die of heart attack. He also suffered from sleep apnoea, which means a person stops breathing in his sleep. Also, Pakistan's poor performances in 2006 (along with accusation of ball-tampering and drug taking) and the shameful exit from the 2007 World Cup could have precipitated a fatal heart attack.

Suicide: This appears to be the least likely possibility. A few hours after the Pakistan shock elimination, he had sent an e-mail to his wife Gill in Cape Town:

> Hi darling, feeling a little depressed currently as you might imagine. I am not sure which is worse, being knocked out in the semi-final at Edgbaston [when South Africa coached by him had lost a thriller to Australia in the 1999 World Cup semi-final] or now in the first round. Our batting performance was abysmal and my worst fears were realised. I could tell the players were for some reason not able to fire themselves up ... Not much more to add I'm afraid but I still love you lots.

He also added in the e-mail that he was looking forward to seeing his family again soon. Not the sort of e-mail a person would send to his wife if he were contemplating suicide.

About 14 hours after pressing the send button on his computer, Woolmer was found dead in his hotel room. He was discovered slumped in the bathroom by a maid after his conspicuous absence from breakfast that morning.

Murder by strangulation or poisoning: Two days after his passing, a post mortem had proved inconclusive and the Jamaican police announced that his death was being treated as suspicious. On 22 March, five days after his passing, a Jamaican journalist Rohan Powell claimed on television that Woolmer had been strangled and the police launched a murder investigation.

Karl Angell, a police spokesman, said that Woolmer's death was owing to asphyxiation due to manual strangulation. 'In these circumstances the matter is now treated by police as murder,' he stated. That very day, *The Gleaner*, a leading Jamaican daily, had a front-page story with a screaming headline: 'Woolmer strangled'.

Apart from the strangulation theory, there was another theory that he was poisoned with a drug called aconite. But why, wondered Paul Newman in *Wisden* 2008. 'Why would anyone want to kill such a respected figure? The spectre of match–fixing has been the biggest threat to cricket's future ever since its existence on a large scale was uncovered in the mid–1990s.'

Sarfraz Nawaz, a Test fast bowler for Pakistan in 1970s, a maverick and the stormy petrel of Pakistan cricket, said that Woolmer had been killed by 'match–fixing mafias'.

Before his death, Woolmer was writing two books, one on coaching with Tim Noakes and the second an updated version of his autobiography with Ivo Tennant. Was he about to reveal all he knew on match–fixing, having known Hansie Cronje personally and the murky world of Pakistan cricket? Woolmer's co–authors Noakes and Tennant stated that they had not discussed match–fixing in these books.

But was Woolmer thinking about a third book about his time as a coach of Pakistan? He had told Osman Samiuddin, the Pakistan editor of *Cricinfo*, that it would be a story worth telling.

New theories kept popping up but there was a turn around on forensic evidence. Two months after Woolmer's death, police privately admitted that their pathology was wrong and on 12 June, Lucius Thomas, the commissioner of the Jamaica Constabulary Force, announced that the investigation had concluded that Bob Woolmer had died of natural causes and was not murdered as indicated by the earlier post mortem report.

Three independent pathologists' reports commissioned by the police had found that the initial conclusion of manual strangulation was incorrect. Toxicology tests also revealed no evidence of poisoning. The findings of the pathologists, and of Scotland Yard detectives who had visited Jamaica to assist with the investigation, were reported in the weeks leading up to the announcement. The forensic reports suggested that Woolmer suffered from health problems, including an enlarged heart and diabetes, which may have contributed to his death.

On 6 November that year, coroner Patrick Murphy asked for further tests to be carried out on samples taken from Woolmer's body following discrepancies in the toxicology reports by scientists from the Caribbean and the UK.

After hearing 26 days of evidence, the jury at the inquest returned an open verdict, refusing to rule out the controversial strangulation theory put forward by pathologist Dr Ere Seshaiah.

In cricketing language it was a draw, one can draw one's own conclusions—a true to life whodunnit or didn't–do–it mystery.

A tragedy of a different dimension struck the cricket world four and half years after the Woolmer death. It was another shocker, the passing of Peter Roebuck. The news hit me personally as Roebuck was my favourite cricket writer and a friend.

To die at a relatively young age of 55 is sad, but to commit suicide by throwing oneself from the sixth floor of the Southern Sun Hotel in Cape Town is beyond belief.

Almost a year has passed since hearing the news of his plunge but I am still in a state of shock because we always got along well. I well remember pleasantries and banters with him at the Sydney Cricket Ground (SCG) Press Box. He said tongue–in–cheek that I frequent the Press Boxes not to see Test matches but to savour the samousas, an Indian delicacy served at teatime. He even mentioned the samousas when he wrote a Foreword for my cricket book *Heroes of 100 Tests*. He honoured me by asking statistical facts and acknowledged my name in the next day's *Sydney Morning Herald*.

No human being is perfect and I had been told about his other side, the dark side. Not being judgemental, I looked at his humane and charitable side, his helping those in need, providing education to those who could not afford it. He was always chuffed when I told him that I enjoyed his witty metaphors and that he was among my three favourite writers, the others being P.G. Wodehouse and Ray Robinson.

Jonathan Agnew, England's former Test cricketer and now a cricket writer, tweeted: 'My God, just heard about Peter Roebuck. Loved working with him. [He was] incisive, erudite and funny.'

The shock of Peter's passing was more profound because I heard the news minutes after I read his article in the *Sun–Herald* that morning. The last paragraph of his final article appears eerie in view of the shocking tragedy that happened a few hours later in the Southern Sun Hotel Newlands. To quote the last paragraph of his story, 'Mind you, a lot can happen in a week. It just did.' Yes, in retrospect it just did!

Much has been written on Peter Roebuck, the Somerset batsman who scored 17 558 runs at 37.27 making 33 centuries (highest score 221 not out) and 93 fifties besides taking 72 wickets and 162 catches in 335 first-class matches spanning from 1974 to 1991, the classy writer of many analytical columns and books, and an enigmatic person. He was Master of Law from Cambridge University and captained it, as also the county Somerset. He was also the skipper of England A team against Holland.

Spiro Zavos wrote on the Roar website, 'Quite simply, he [Roebuck] was the best writer about cricket of his generation. His articles were invariably gems of essays, full of insight, humour and compassion for the trials and tribulations of the players at all levels of the game.'

In a perceptive article in the *Sydney Morning Herald*, Greg Baum wrote:

It is possible to say where he [Roebuck] came from, but not where he belonged. After moving from England he kept houses in Bondi [Sydney] and Pietermaritzburg... He was an Australian citizen who cherished his work for Fairfax and the ABC. He played the Pom in Australia and the maverick in England. But he perhaps found his life's work in South Africa, where he created a community of forty underprivileged South African and Zimbabwean boys and spent pretty much every cent he earned putting them through school. He talked endlessly about them. They were on his mind at the end.

As Roebuck was estranged from his family, the underprivileged Zimbabwean and South African boys became his family.

He played for a Somerset that included mega stars Viv Richards, Joel Garner and Ian Botham. Appointed captain of Somerset in 1985, Roebuck thought that Richards and Garner were not giving off their best for Somerset and advised the Committee to replace them with New Zealander Martin Crowe. *Wisden* 2012 recalled in Roebuck's obituary, 'The upshot was disaster: the news came as a bombshell and Botham stormed out in protest.' This resulted in a bitter relationship between Roebuck and Botham and the repercussions went on for many years.

Roebuck was also at the centre of controversy in 2001, when he received a suspended jail sentence for common assault after beating three teenage cricketers across their bare buttocks with a cane.

Let's revisit the 2011 Cape Town tragedy. According to *The New Age*, Roebuck had met his Zimbabwean accuser a week before arriving in Cape Town to cover South Africa's Test against Australia.

The newspaper added that it was believed that Roebuck arranged to meet the young man to discuss the possibility of helping him attend university. But he allegedly tried to seduce him and have sex with him against his will. 'The man reportedly went to Claremont police station and laid charges of indecent assault against Roebuck,' wrote *The New Age*. The newspaper claimed the broadcaster was due to be arrested but asked to change his clothes before leaving the hotel.

In desperation, Roebuck phoned fellow cricket journalist Jim Maxwell from his hotel room to help find him a lawyer and contact a group of underprivileged boys he had been supporting near his South African home. 'Can you come down to my room quickly, I've got a problem,' he asked Maxwell in a desperate phone call that night.

Minutes later, with the uniformed officer still in the room about to make an arrest, Roebuck plunged 70 feet to his death, hitting an awning as he fell. Paramedics were called to the hotel, a short walk from the Newlands cricket ground, and Roebuck was pronounced dead at the scene.

Police seized items from his hotel room, including a laptop computer.

A distraught Maxwell, one of the last people to see Roebuck alive, gave a statement to police the next day. 'Things happen. As far as I could see at the Test, there wasn't a problem,' Maxwell said. 'He was a person who had a great sense of humanity and caring. That was Peter. There were a lot of other things about him, but we've lost a wonderful friend and supporter.' He described Roebuck as 'one of the outstanding writers on the game of cricket'.

On Roebuck's death, Maxwell said:

I'm sure what happened was triggered by the visit of the police and the fact that they were going to charge him with an alleged sexual assault, which meant he was going to be detained and would then have to appear in court on Monday. This is what I discovered when I went to his room after he made a very agitated, dramatic, despairing phone call to my room. He was absolutely on edge.

When I arrived the detective came out and filled me in on the details. It was then that I asked if I could speak to him [Roebuck] and the detective said 'well, just for a moment', because clearly they didn't want their case compromised in some way, I suppose, by what he may have said to me. So I only had a few moments with him. He was desperate to get in touch with all those students that were in his care in Pietermaritzburg.

Later, the police spokesman, Captain Frederick Van Wyk, confirmed that Roebuck's death was treated as suicide.

A charitable person, he gave his best for the unprivileged youth in Zimbabwe, India, Pakistan and elsewhere through his work with the LBW (Learning for a Better World) Trust. I enjoyed the friendly discussions I had with Peter at the SCG Press Box and the light-hearted e-mails we exchanged when he was not in Australia.

The press boxes around the cricketing world do not look the same without him and his straw hat.

PETER ROEBUCK WAS ENIGMATIC AS A person and his prose was full of clever epigrams. Here are my favourite Roebuckisms:

'[Steve] Waugh's first hundred drained the life from his opponents. His second buried them. Mark Waugh is a rose to his brother's thorn'—said after an injured Steve Waugh's gallant centuries in both innings of the 1997 Manchester Ashes Test.

'In [Wasim] Akram's hands a ball does not so much talk as sing. With a flick of the wrist and an arm that flashes past his ears like a thought through a child's brain he pushes the ball across the batsmen and makes it dip back wickedly late. Akram's career has been not so much a career as a merry-go-round. A compelling figure, he has the grin of a playboy, the face of a gangster and the powers of a cricketing genius.'

'Born in the West Indies and raised in England, [Gordon] Greenidge had a foot in both camps and a tent in neither.'

His writings, in many ways, encapsulate the Peter Roebuck persona.

MINI-
CONFLICTS AND
CONTROVERSIES

DON BRADMAN V. JACK FINGLETON AND BILL O'REILLY

There were differences between Sir Donald Bradman and some of his teammates on religious grounds. Bradman was an Anglican and many of the others—Jack Fingleton, Bill O'Reilly, Clarrie Grimmett, Stan McCabe—were Catholics. But there were other differences too.

Both Fingleton and O'Reilly had the highest opinion of Bradman as a batsman but had personal issues with him. According to Alan Eason in *The A–Z of Bradman* (2008), Fingleton was critical of 'The Don' for receiving prize money and not sharing it with his teammates, not even shouting them a drink.

Eason wrote, 'Fingleton was notably critical of Bradman's ploy against Bodyline of stepping away to the leg side and playing to the near–vacant off–side.' Fingleton alleged that Bradman did this solely to avoid being stuck and was against the interest of his team. Bradman denied this vehemently in his autobiography *Farewell to Cricket* (1950).

When the famous words spoken by Australia's skipper Bill Woodfull to England's manager Plum Warner during the Bodyline series, 'There's two teams out there, and only one of them's playing cricket' were leaked to the press, Fingleton, a journalist, was blamed. Fingleton denied this hotly and blamed Bradman for this leak, repeating this charge in his book *Batting from Memory* (1981). Bradman called Fingleton's claim 'a lie'.

Bradman and O'Reilly also had a love–hate relationship. The admiration between the two legends of the game started in 1925–26 when 17–year–old Bradman hit 234 runs for Bowral (NSW) against the village of Wingello in a famous encounter with O'Reilly, who was then 20 years of age. The two Aussie icons went on to play for Australia for many years. To Bradman, O'Reilly was the greatest spin bowler, 'the daddy of them all'. And to O'Reilly, Bradman was the greatest

> *Both Fingleton and O'Reilly had the highest opinion of Bradman as a batsman but had personal issues with him. According to Alan Eason in* The A–Z of Bradman *(2008), Fingleton was critical of 'The Don' for receiving prize money and not sharing it with his teammates, not even shouting them for a drink.*

batsman, 'the Babe Ruth of cricket'.

But they had a fallout when O'Reilly criticised Bradman for the dropping of Grimmett for the 1938 tour of England and also for interfering with bowlers in field-placing. Bradman strongly refuted both these charges.

When Bradman was out for a duck in his last Test innings against England at The Oval, and could not achieve a Test average of 100, O'Reilly and Fingleton, who were in The Oval press box, could not conceal their delight, wrote Simon Wilde in his book *Number One: The World's Best Batsmen and Bowlers* (1998). England's cricket columnist Jim Swanton had revealed to Bradman's biographer Charles Williams in 1996 that when Don was bowled for a second-ball duck in his final Test innings, 'I thought they [Fingleton and O'Reilly who were in the press box as journalists] were going to have a stroke—they were laughing so much.'

O'Reilly later admitted to friends that he had laughed, but only at the incongruity of the occasion. Bradman wrote to Williams in 1995, 'O'Reilly nakedly exposes the disloyalty I had to endure during my years as Australian captain, a disloyalty based on jealousy and religion.'

Bradman wrote a personal letter to me in July 1995:

Thank you for the piece you wrote about Ernie Toshack. I had in fact seen it before in WCM [Wisden Cricket Monthly] and was touched by the nice comments he made about me [regarding not interfering with the bowler in field placing]. It was of considerable comfort to me coming so soon after the despicable remarks made by O'Reilly in the earlier WCM. Ernie was always a good friend.

THE ECCENTRIC MR CONINGHAM

The Protestant–Roman Catholic conflict also coloured the Arthur Coningham story. You may well ask, Arthur Coningham who? He was an eccentric and unique Australian all-rounder who played one Test in 1894–95 in Melbourne.

But what a debut! He took a wicket off his first ball, the first bowler to do so in Test annals. He opened the attack and dismissed England's opener Archie MacLaren off his first ball. He took 2 for 17 and 0 for 59, scored 10 and 3 and was never selected in a Test again. Despite being bowled out for 75 in the first innings, England won the Test by 94 runs.

Overconfident and volatile, Coningham was no-balled when bowling to

England captain Andrew Stoddart. In annoyance, he deliberately threw the next one at the batsman.

In 35 first-class matches for Queensland and New South Wales from 1892 to 1898, the left-handed Coningham scored 896 runs at 15.73, highest score 151 for Queensland against New South Wales in 1895–96 and took 112 wickets at 23.24 as an opening bowler. He captured five wickets in an innings seven times, his best figures being 6 for 38 for New South Wales against Victoria in 1896–97.

He had a quirky record. In a Brisbane competition match in 1890–91, he scored *all* 26 runs for his club team, Stanley. You may well say that he gave his 100 per cent!

In 1900, he made headlines in the Australian media when the Protestant Coningham sued Roman Catholic Father O'Haran, administrator of St Mary's Cathedral in Sydney, for allegedly having an affair with his wife. This 'scandal' aroused strong religious passions.

When his solicitor walked out, Coningham conducted his own case, revolver at his hip, although he lost it. It was the conspiracy sensation of 1900.

Coningham was featured in Cyril Pearl's book *Wild Men of Sydney*. Even outside cricket he was an all-rounder—a Jack of all trades. A chemist by profession he was also a hairdresser, a tobacconist and a bookmaker. Besides cricket he was adept in athletics, billiards, rowing and rugby.

A popular and whimsical character, he once amused himself and spectators by collecting a few sticks and lighting a fire to keep himself warm when fielding during a match in Blackpool, England in 1893. That year 'Conny' received a medal for saving a boy's life in the Thames.

He died aged 75 in a mental home but his son, Sir Arthur Coningham, became an RAF Air Marshal.

LARRIKIN MATTHEWS'S WILD TEST DEBUT

Greg 'Mo' Matthews is a colourful character, an Aussie larrikin. Frank and outspoken, there are no shades of gray about him. Ambidextrous, he batted left-hand and bowled right-arm off-spin. In 33 Tests between 1983 and 1992 he scored 1849 runs at 41.08 with four centuries and took 61 wickets at 48.22.

His most memorable match was the tied Test between Australia and India in Chennai in 1986. He took five wickets in each innings, trapping Indian batsman

Maninder Singh lbw to tie the Test, only the second in history. When other players were nearly collapsing of heat stroke, Matthews wore a sweater throughout this match. Why? 'This was to show to my mates that it was not that unbearably hot,' he told me. 'Call it a psychological ploy.'

He made a unique Test debut. It was against Pakistan on the Melbourne Cricket Ground on Boxing Day 1983. Matthews tells it in his own words:

I was almost a kid then, only 24 with experience of barely ten first-class matches. I was nervous, playing my first Test match in front of a huge crowd at the MCG. I had worn my brother's favourite sweater for good luck. As I tried to enter the Players Room, a gate-keeper stopped me asking for my pass. He did not believe me when I said I was playing in this Test. 'You can't come in', he insisted. As I was getting desperately late for the Test, I jumped the turnstile and he caught hold of my lucky sweater and tore it.

The match has pleasant memories as I scored 75 runs, adding 185 runs with Graham Yallop for the seventh wicket and took four wickets in the match, including the scalps of opener Mudassar Nazar and classy batsman Zaheer Abbas in the second innings. But did I receive plaudits for these performances?

Three days later I received a phone call for a 6.30 a.m. meeting when I was hit with a fine of $1000 for jumping the turnstile. Senior cricketers who should have made me—a newcomer—feel welcome made fun of me and I was infuriated. Later the fine was reduced to $500 and I was paid only $910 out of my match fee of $1410.

LAWRY V. INDIAN PHOTOGRAPHERS

Five weeks after the 1969 Bombay Test, described in flaming detail in chapter 9, the fourth Test at Eden Gardens, Calcutta (now Kolkata) was played. Bill Lawry's morale was down having lost the previous Test in Delhi to India by seven wickets. The series was now level one–all and single-minded Lawry wanted to win this Test.

Kolkata Tests are noted for riots and this one was no exception. On the fourth day, Australia needed 39 runs to win and was 0 for 7 when hundreds of spectators spilled on the playing area after being pelted by fruits from the stands above and there was a 15-minute break in play.

During this delay, several photographers entered the field to get close-up photos of Lawry and his opening batting partner Keith Stackpole. With victory on his mind, an impatient Lawry pushed away an intrusive photographer who fell heavily, leading to accusations of assault. This inflamed an already tense situation.

India's columnist Rajan Bala gave a different version about the photographer episode in his book *Kiwis and Kangaroos — India 1969* (1970). 'Skipper Lawry with the Bombay conflagration still fresh in his mind was all "nerves" when a photographer came too close to take a shot. The Australian version of Pinnochio ran after the fellow and knocked him over. It was a horrible sight.'

This is how Ian Chappell, who had scored 99 in this Test, recalled the incident in a recent personal interview with me:

> Australia only required a few runs to win and India's captain 'Tiger' Pataudi was keen to get the game finished that night. The crowd was giving 'Tiger' and the Indian side a hard time and things were being thrown from the higher reaches of the stadium and this forced the fans below to seek refuge on the field.
>
> When a few photographers came onto the ground to get shots, Bill and 'Stacky' [Stackpole] asked them to leave the field. They refused and when one of them wandered too close to the pitch Bill pushed him away with his hand. The guy fell and unfortunately there was a shot in the paper the next morning with Bill standing over the guy and it was reported that Lawry had hit the photographer with his bat.
>
> This is rubbish. Bill was never one to be put off by a riot and he always did his best to keep the game going when there was trouble. He was so protective of his wicket that I can understand him being angered by the thought of anyone damaging the pitch, he would've been thinking that this could lead to him losing his wicket.

Australia won by ten wickets but after the Test the Australian team bus was stoned as it made its way to the airport.

IAN CHAPPELL V. GLENN TURNER

The 1973–74 Test series between Australia and New Zealand in New Zealand was memorable for both countries. In the first Test in Wellington, Ian and Greg Chappell became the only brothers to score centuries together in both the innings; Ian 145 and 121, Greg 247 not out and 133. Greg was at his majestic best in both the innings.

But it is the second Test in Christchurch a week later that was more dramatic.

As R.T. Brittenden wrote in *Wisden* 1975, 'New Zealand cricket has known no greater occasion than 13 March 1974 when a Test against Australia was won for the first time at the sixth time of asking.' The Kiwis had to wait 28 years for this memorable moment.

This Christchurch Test is also remembered for an unsavoury incident between Australian captain Ian Chappell and New Zealand opener Glenn Turner. Late on the fourth day, New Zealander Brian Hastings hit a boundary that was signalled as a six by umpire R. Monteith.

Sportingly, Turner pointed out to the umpire that the ball had bounced over the line and was not a six. As Turner told me recently, 'Before Monteith could correct the signal, Ian Chappell ran up from his slip position. I began to assure Ian that the error was being corrected, but Ian spoke forcibly to me.'

Turner and several of the other New Zealand players asked, through their captain Bevan Congdon, for an apology. Chappell said he would not apologise and added that what happened on the field of play ended there.

But as New Zealand won by five wickets and Turner became the first from his country to hit centuries in both innings (101 and 110 not out), he felt ten feet tall. Both his centuries were special to him.

He was 99 not out at stumps on the second day and was on that score for 34 balls. Needing 228 runs for a win, the home team were five down for 206 but Turner guided them to a well-deserved victory with an unbeaten hundred on the final day.

GREIG'S GROVEL SNUB BACKFIRES

England's captain Tony Greig raised eyebrows and heckles when previewing the 1976 series against the West Indies. To raise England's morale, he suggested on television that the West Indies cricketers were temperamental. He added that they were not as good as they were made out. If they get on top they are magnificent cricketers but if they are down, they grovel, and with the help of his teammates, he intended to make them grovel.

The outcry was instantaneous. The word 'grovel' has sinister connotations for West Indian people as many of them have slave ancestry. Moreover, apartheid and the Gleneagles Agreement were burning issues then. So a white South African uttering the word 'grovel' to the West Indians was a big 'no-no'.

The dreaded West Indian fast bowlers took great delight in bowling bouncers at 150 plus kilometres–per–hour when Greig came to the wicket and the West Indians in the crowd were ecstatic when he was dismissed. Except in the Leeds' Test where he scored 116 and 76 not out, Greig failed miserably, averaging 30.37 with the bat and 67.20 with the ball.

This Christchurch Test is also remembered for an unsavoury incident between Australian captain Ian Chappell and New Zealand opener Glenn Turner. Late on the fourth day, New Zealander Brian Hastings hit a boundary that was signalled as a six by umpire R. Monteith.

On the other hand, in the one–sided Test series, Viv Richards hit 829 runs at 118.42, Gordon Greenidge 592 at 65.77 and Roy Fredericks 517 at 57.44. Also, the Windies speed aces Michael Holding and Andy Roberts captured 28 wickets each at 12.71 and 19.17.

'Who's grovelling now?' asked his critics. 'Okay, so I'm grovelling now,' joked Greig, in a front–page story in *The Sun*, going on his knees as the crowd cheered.

He commented three decades later:

Anyone who wants to suggest it was my South African background that was behind my comment and put any racist tone to this thing just doesn't know me. None of the West Indies players ever confronted me about my comments at the start of the series; they were just faster and nastier whenever I came to the crease.

LEVER'S VASELINE STRIPS DRAMA

England's pace bowler John Lever made a dream Test debut in Delhi against India in December 1976 with figures of 7 for 46 and 3 for 24—England won by an innings. But the next month in the third Test in Madras (now Chennai) he was in trouble when it was alleged that he had used vaseline on the ball to help it swing.

The vaseline incident happened on the second day of the Test just as India's innings was coming to an end and he had taken five wickets. Umpire Judah Reuben reported that he was carrying on his person a strip of surgical gauze impregnated with vaseline. The umpire considered this to be a breach of Law 46.

The MCC management conceded that there was vaseline on the strip of gauze but explained that on a hot and humid day both Lever and Bob Willis suffered from smarting eyes due to perspiration running into them from the forehead. On the advice of team physiotherapist, Bernard Thomas, they went out wearing the gauze strips to divert the trickle of sweat away from the eyes.

There were two explanations for the presence of a gauze strip on the ground. Umpire Reuben said that it came adrift while Lever was delivering the ball. The team management claimed that Lever found it a hindrance and discarded it himself.

Former Test great and the MCC manager, Ken Barrington, agreed that there was a technical breach of the law governing 'fair and unfair play' but the offence was completely unintentional. At a press conference the following day, Barrington and skipper Tony Greig stressed that the gauze strips were not worn until after lunch and by then the England team had made such inroads into the Indian innings that such unfair methods were unnecessary.

Greig recently recalled that incident:

What happened was that John Lever had a habit of taking sweat from his brow, which is perfectly legitimate as long as it is only sweat. However, he did mix the vaseline-impregnated gauze with some of the sweat on his brow, because he had this habit of going straight across his brow. So, purely by accident, he found himself with a slippery hand and, as a result of that, he decided to get rid of that gauze. He took it off his eyes and put it down at the base of the stumps in front of the umpire. This was picked up by the umpire, who recognised that it was a foreign substance, and of course that's how it got out of control.

There is absolutely no doubt in my mind that this was an inadvertent mistake by our physiotherapist and that we weren't, in any way, trying to pull the wool over [India's captain] Bishan Bedi and his team's eyes. In fact, had we been doing that then why would Lever put the gauze down at the base of the stumps? So that's basically what happened.

Bedi added fuel to the fire by stating that even after the Delhi Test when Lever had captured ten wickets, he had suspicions that a polishing agent of some kind had been used.

Greig forcefully denied this allegation saying:

Bishan Bedi was under a tremendous amount of pressure at that time because the team was 2–0 down, and after that Test match 3–0 down. There was plenty of speculation whether he would hang onto the captaincy. He was, I think, grasping at straws at that time. In any event, the explanation from Kenny Barrington and me, and indeed the response from Lord's got behind my explanation that this was a mistake. I am quite happy to admit right now that it should never have happened, but it did, and there is nothing much we could do about it.

HYPERACTIVE BOTHAM

Ian Botham was one of the greatest all-rounders in cricket history, being as at July 2012 the only one to achieve the Test triple of 5000 runs, 300 wickets and 100 catches. A character of the game, he was according to India's opening batsman and good friend Sunil Gavaskar:

The craziest cricketer I've known. He was an absolute terror in the [Somerset] dressing room because he could not sit still. If he did not find anything to do he would dip his teaspoon in a pot of hot, boiling water and while you were sitting unawares, he would try to cause burns on your hands with the spoon or just a lighted matchstick.

In other words, he was a hyperactive prankster.

By the mid-1980s, Botham was as much the property of the tabloids as Shane Warne was in the 2000s, only he often gifted the high-octane fuel for their stories. According to Martin Williamson in *Cricinfo*:

In May 1986 he admitted to the Mail on Sunday that he had smoked cannabis, weeks after returning from a Caribbean tour remembered more for off-the-field headlines than anything on it. The irony was that the one-off article was part of an agreement resulting from legal action Botham had taken against the newspaper. The establishment spluttered, held a seven-hour hearing and then suspended him for two months

Botham later admitted, 'I don't think I have ever been quite so drunk in my life.' Controversies chased him in many continents. The legendary English all-rounder had a three year contract to play for Queensland in the late-1980s but selfdestructed himself by his drinking sprees and was sacked by Queensland after just three months in 1988. Ken Piesse details Botham's misadventures that year in Australia in *Cricket's Greatest Scandals* (2001), 'After a one-day game, he and Dennis Lillee were accused of creating mayhem in the Old Scotch Collegians dressing rooms at the historic Launceston Cricket Ground; glasses and light fittings being broken and an honour board damaged.'

This was only a prelude to more serious offences, the most outrageous occurring during a 4-hour air flight from Tullamarine to Perth where he again cornered headlines. Ignoring Queensland captain Allan Border's 'no-drinks' directive, he became involved in heated arguments with teammates with four-letter words flying faster than the plane.

When a passenger turned round and said, 'C'mon fellas, keep it down', Botham put his hands on the complainer's shoulders and turned him around. According to the passenger Botham had held him firmly by the scalp and hair and shook his head from side to side, uttering obscenities.

Within an hour of landing in Perth, police arrested him, formally charging him with assault and offensive behaviour. Lillee bailed him out with a A$5000 surety. Botham later pleaded guilty and was fined A$800. He was also fired by the Queensland Cricket Association.

Unrepentant, he later said, 'As far as I was concerned, a trifling little matter had grown out of all proportion. I knew I had powerful enemies at Queensland.'

Despite his trespasses, Ian Botham should be remembered for his mighty deeds on the field, especially the Leeds 1981 Ahes Test, which England won thanks to Botham's all-round excellence. It was probably the biggest turn around in cricket history. England were forced to follow on 227 runs behind and were 7 for 135, still 92 in arrears, when he hit an unbeaten 149 and England won by 18 runs.

In June 2007, he was knighted by the Queen for his cricketing achievements and his commendable efforts in raising funds for leukaemia research.

ATHERTON CAUGHT WITH DIRT IN POCKET

Rarely is a Test match both historic and controversial. The Lord's Test between England and South Africa in July 1994 was one.

Till the early 1990s it was stressed by the Western writers that only sub-continent cricketers tampered with the ball, the unspoken implication being that an Englishman would never stoop so low. This belief was laid to rest when an English captain was caught on camera in a Test in England with dirt on his fingers.

The Test was of historic importance because it was the first Test played by South Africa in England in almost three decades because of their exile. To celebrate their comeback the visitors won by 356 runs with a day to spare after dismissing England for a paltry 99 in the final innings.

However, the headlines were full of the dirt-in-pocket scandal involving young England captain Michael Atherton. He was seen by the television cameras taking his hand out of his pocket and rubbing it across the ball before passing it back to the bowler. The British media were shocked by what they saw and exploded in a frenzy of righteous indignation. 'Barely a year after assuming the England captaincy at the tender age of 25, Michael Atherton found himself being crushed by the weight of the moral majority,' wrote Andrew Miller.

Atherton was called before the match referee, the former Australian Test batsman, Peter Burge to explain his action. Had he broken Law 42.5—using an artificial substance to alter the condition of the ball? Burge said that he had accepted Atherton's explanation without saying what it was.

But the next day, after further television footage was shown, the incident appeared more sinister. According to *Wisden* 1995, Atherton admitted that he had not told Burge the truth when saying he had nothing in his pocket. Burge was understandably livid. Had he known the full story about the dirt, Burge later said, he would have suspended Atherton for two matches. In all probability, this would have brought about an early end to his tenure as captain.

That evening, Atherton recorded his version of events, as they had unfolded, in his matter-of-fact diary:

> Hot and humid day. Gough is getting some reverse-swing and tells [mid-on and mid-off] to make sure we keep our sweaty hands off the rough side of the ball. Sals [Ian Salisbury] rubs his hands in the footholds of an old pitch on the grandstand side and I put some dust in my pocket from a used pitch on the Tavern side. I use the dust to keep my hands and the ball dry three or four times.

Atherton's defense—and he had a case regardless of the incriminating footage—was that he was not seeking to alter the condition of the dry and roughed-up ball, but maintain the condition it had already reached. Unfortunately, that was not the story he told to referee Burge who presided over that evening's hearing. By his own admission, Atherton was called before the headmaster with a cane and had panicked.

To this day, it is not clear as to what Atherton's intentions were or whether he was contravening the rules, which are suitably ambiguous. Law 42.5 states: 'No one shall rub the ball on the ground, or use any artificial substance, or take any other action to alter the condition of the ball,' and seeing as dust is neither artificial, nor in this particular case, on the ground, the only issue at stake was the third part—altering the condition of the ball. It was on that issue that opinions differ wildly.

STEVE WAUGH V. CURTLY AMBROSE

The red-hot mid-wicket confrontation between 'never-say-never' Steve Waugh and ferociously fast bowler Curtly Ambrose took place during the Port-of-Spain Test between Australia and the West Indies in April 1995.

On a green pitch, covered by grass almost a centimetre long, it appeared as if the Test would finish in three days. And it did. Australia was sent in to bat and was dismissed for 128, Steve Waugh (63 not out) scoring the only 50 of the match. It was one of the toughest innings of his career. He played and missed but carried on despite booing from a parochial crowd. But he lost his temper when he saw the tall 6'7" (201 cms) bowling bouncers at him and coming close to him after his bowling run-up with that menacing glare.

As Waugh writes in his autobiography *Out of My Comfort Zone* (2005), 'So when I saw Ambrose staring intently from close quarters I snapped at him, "What the f— are you looking at?" This was a clear case of the mouth beating the brain to the punch. It was what I was thinking, but saying it took even me by surprise.'

Shocked at Waugh's language (and courage), Ambrose countered by saying, 'Don't cuss me, man.'

Defiantly, Waugh stood his ground exchanging glares. Nothing witty or inventive came to his mind, rather another piece of abuse, 'Why don't you go and get f—ed.' Ambrose was wild with anger and an uglier scene was averted when West Indies skipper Richie Richardson stepped in, held Ambrose with his wrist with both hands and pulled him away.

Ambrose bowled with fire within his belly but could not dismiss Waugh in either innings. However, he was adjudged the Man of the Match with figures of 5 for 45 and 4 for 20 as the Windies won by nine wickets.

This series saw the changing of guards as Australia, under Mark Taylor, defeated the 'invincible' West Indians 2–1. The Windies had lost a Test series for the first time after 15 years of total domination. The man behind Australia's resurgence was Steve Waugh, who amassed 429 runs at 107.25 in four Tests in that series, climaxing with a double century in the final Test in Kingston.

When inducted into the ICC Hall of Fame in September 2011, Ambrose recalled his mid–pitch, eye–to–eye altercation with Steve Waugh:

I'm not one of those guys who really got into any confrontations with cricketers. My stare does a lot for me. I always believed that I prefer to let the ball do all the talking for me. The incident with Steve Waugh ... I always respected him highly and it was the heat of the moment really. There was very fierce competition between Australia and the West Indies.

We were down 0–1 in the series, there was a bit of pressure and we were on the brink of losing our number one tag. He just said something to me that I didn't like. I thought he should have showed me a little more respect. My impression was to let it go but then thinking about it I said no. I decided to retaliate a bit. In that heat of the moment I really wanted to physically beat him. But the fine thing is it happened on the day, for a brief moment, and ended there. Nothing else was said after that.

WORLD CUP RIOT IN OH KOLKATA

The 1996 World Cup in the Indian sub–continent started with a controversy before a ball was bowled. Australia and the West Indies refused to play in Sri Lanka because a fortnight previously there was a bomb blast in Colombo, where they were scheduled to play their matches. It may be added that the Australian cricketers were also uncomfortable about visiting Sri Lanka after their acrimonious Test series in Australia a few months earlier as detailed in chapter 20.

Sri Lanka went on to win their only World Cup by beating Australia in the Final at Lahore. However, the headlines were dominated by the riot in Kolkata during the semi–final clash between India and Sri Lanka at Eden Gardens, Calcutta (now Kolkata). It appeared anything but a Garden of Eden that night on 13 March, with bottles being thrown on the ground and fire–lighting in the stands.

It was India's spineless batting that led to disillusionment among almost

100 000 spectators who had paid good money to see a contest between two strong teams. India's captain Mohammad Azharuddin surprised the critics by electing to field after winning the toss on a good batting pitch. He knew that Sri Lanka were good chasers so he decided to bat last.

The match started well for India as Sri Lanka lost their in-form opening batsmen Sanath Jayasuriya and Romesh Kaluwitharana to speedster Javagal Sreenath with only one run on the scoreboard. They became 3 for 35 and 4 for 85 and it seemed Azharuddin's gamble of sending Sri Lanka in to bat had worked. But Aravinda de Silva and Roshan Mahanama batted brilliantly and they ended up with 8 for 251.

India started their reply promisingly with Sachin Tendulkar, following his tidy bowling spell of 10-1-34-2, scored 65 before he was stumped. But the other batsmen failed and after 34.1 overs, India was on her knees at 8 for 120, still 132 runs needed off 15.5 overs with only two wickets in hand.

Angered by an Indian collapse of seven wickets for 22 runs after Tendulkar's departure, some Indian supporters threw bottles on the outfield and set fires to the seating. Match referee Clive Lloyd took the team off for 15 minutes, attempted a restart and then awarded the match to Sri Lanka by default. No one questioned this decision, as winning was impossible for India.

Many home fans were embarrassed by the crowd's unforgivable behaviour and raised a banner reading, 'Congratulation Sri Lanka—we are sorry.'

The presentation ceremony went ahead as if nothing had happened with de Silva adjudged Man of the Match. But the smoking backdrop told the story of this wild World Cup encounter. Forgetting this traumatic semi-final, Sri Lanka went on to defeat Australia in the Final by seven wickets in Lahore four days later, de Silva again dominating with a brilliant and unbeaten 107.

BITING BALLS, NOT BULLETS — AFRIDI STYLE

Pakistani all-rounder Shahid Afridi is a man of many parts who somehow does not make one whole. He can win a match off his own bat hitting sixes all over the park or capture wickets with his versatile leg-spinners off successive overs and is aptly nicknamed 'Boom Boom'. But more often he would disappoint his ardent fans by doing incredibly silly things, such as biting a ball as if it were an apple!

This happened on 31 January 2010, in a one-day international at Perth. After trailing Australia 0–4, Pakistan played their last match of a frustrating season under a new captain, Afridi. And for once they were offering the hosts some resistance.

After totalling 212, the tourists were on their way towards their first international win of the summer when Australia was losing quick wickets. But the excitement of an approaching close finish was marred by the sight of Afridi biting the ball, a novel form of ball-tampering.

After totalling 212, the tourists were on their way towards their first international win of the summer when Australia was losing quick wickets. But the excitement of an approaching close finish was marred by the sight of Afridi biting the ball, a novel form of ball-tampering.

He said immediately after the match, 'I was trying to smell it and [find out] how it was feeling.' However, he later admitted: 'I am ashamed. I did it in the heat of the moment as the match was a close one, but I should not have done that, it's a serious offence.'

He was banned from the next two Twenty20 matches. His significant throw-away line after receiving the punishment was, 'There is no team in the world that does not tamper with the ball.'

Not a stranger to controversies, 'Boom Boom' Afridi was banned for one Test and two ODIs in 2005 for deliberately scuffing up the wicket with his spikes in a match against England in Faisalabad.

As if the ball-biting episode was not revolting enough, a drunken spectator had tackled Pakistan fielder Khalid Latif in the middle a little before Afridi's ball-biting spectacle. Former Australian Test fast bowler and a radio summariser during the Perth ODI in 2010, Terry Alderman winced as he recalled his own shoulder-wrecking clash in a Perth Ashes Test on 13 November 1982.

About twenty spectators had then invaded the playing area on the second afternoon. Punched from behind, Alderman chased his assailant with a flying tackle but dislocated his shoulder so badly that the injury ended his first-class season. The assailant was a semi-drunk unemployed teenager, an English migrant named Garry Donnison.

'I can't remember a lot of how I fell ... but I was immediately aware I was injured. It was very painful indeed,' Alderman said.

IT RINGS A BELL

The rollercoaster Trent Bridge Test between England and India struck a heavy rock on the stroke of teatime on the third day, 31 July 2011. England's centurion batsman Ian Bell's carelessness almost resulted in a big controversy.

This is how the Test was progressing before the controversial Bell incident. Sent in to bat, England scored 221 after being 6 for 88 at one stage. On the second day, India was in a commanding position when they were 4 for 267, a lead of 46 with six wickets in hand and Rahul Dravid and Yuvraj Singh were batting confidently. Inexplicably they collapsed for 288, losing their last six wickets for 21 runs; tall, baby-faced speedster Stuart Broad captured 6 for 46. Then it was England all the way, led by a splendid innings by Bell. He was on 137 when he left his crease thinking it was teatime. He wrongly presumed that his partner Eoin Morgan had hit a four. Actually, Praveen Kumar had stopped the ball in the deep.

By laws of cricket, India was correct in appealing for a run-out when Bell was out of his crease when stumps were broken. The umpire Asad Rauf had not called 'over' for a break. By the rules of the game, the two umpires, Rauf and Marais Erasmus, were also correct in declaring Bell run out because the ball was not dead.

However, it was the spirit of the game that put cricket followers in two minds. Obviously Bell, and probably his batting partner Morgan, had thought that it was teatime and were returning to the pavilion.

Full praise should go to India's skipper M.S. Dhoni for withdrawing the appeal during the tea interval after discussions with his teammates. Bell was allowed to resume his splendid innings and a huge controversy was avoided.

The Bell incident of July 2011 'rang a bell'. A similar incident had occurred almost four decades ago in the Port-of-Spain Test of February 1974. And the 'villain' of the piece was England's all-rounder, the tall Tony Greig.

It was the first Test of the series between the West Indies and England. England was dismissed for 131 and the home team replied with 392. In between there was an incident similar to Bell's in the more recent Trent Bridge Test.

Off the last ball of the second day of the Port-of-Spain Test, an extraordinary incident took place that led to angry crowd reactions followed by a long meeting between the officials of both teams. This is how it happened.

When West Indian batsman Bernard Julien played the last ball of the second day down the pitch, Greig picked it up. Then, observing that Alvin Kallicharran (on 142 then) was out of the crease, he threw down the stumps and appealed. Kallicharran was declared run out by umpire Sang Hue and the crowd was furious.

After prolonged dialogue and consultations between captains Mike Denness (England) and Rohan Kanhai (West Indies), umpires Sang Hue and Ralph Gosein, and administrators, the appeal was withdrawn. Greig and England's manager Donald Carr apologised and peace was restored. Kallicharran resumed his batting, like Bell did 37 years later.

Wisden 1975 add that Greig's action was spontaneous and no malice was intended. It was also emphasised that umpire Sang Hue was correct in his decision in Port-of-Spain, Trinidad, as were Asad Rauf and Marais Erasmus in Trent Bridge, Nottingham.

Kallicharran took his score to 158. Coincidentally, Bell also went on to score 159 that evening.

India lost the Trent Bridge Test by a big margin of 319 runs but they showed sportsmanship. Dean Wilson wrote in *Wisden* 2012:

> When the geopolitical relations between England and India is studied in lecture theatres in 50 years' time, it is just possible the Trent Bridge Test will earn a passing mention. India's act of sportsmanship in recalling Bell, who had been legitimately-if controversially – run out from the last ball before tea on the third day, was as generous as it was diplomatic.

And the 'boos' from the crowd when Bell was declared out turned to 'cheers' when India's skipper M.S. Dhoni reinstated Bell.

THE CLARKE — KATICH ALTERCATION

What is now remembered as the 'Pup-Kat spat' happened shortly after the exciting Sydney Test between Australia and South Africa on 7 January 2009. Australia won with just 5 minutes and ten balls left in the game. It was the third and final Test of the series and the visitors had already won it 2–0 when winning the Melbourne Test a weeks earlier.

Australia had to win in Sydney to retain their No.1 Test ranking. With Michael Clark hitting 138, Australia totalled 445—South Africa trailed by 118 runs. A fast delivery from Mitchell Johnson put the visiting captain Graeme Smith in hospital with a broken hand. Sensing victory, Ricky Ponting declared Australia's second innings at 4 for 257, setting South Africa 376 to win on a deteriorating pitch.

Australia thought they had won the match when the opponents were 9 for 257 as skipper Smith was so badly injured that he could not tie his shoelace let alone don the pads. But as only 36 minutes were remaining to draw the match, the captain courageously struggled to the crease, his left hand in plaster. The crowd stood and roared in appreciation. He lasted 26 minutes scoring 3, adding 15 runs with Makhaya Ntini. Australia won by 103 runs but the cheers were for the gallant Smith.

There was the usual victory celebration in the Australian dressing room. But an unsavoury incident spoilt the party. Vice-captain Clarke and Simon Katich were involved in an altercation. *The Daily Telegraph* reported that the players argued over the singing of the team song, 'Beneath the Southern Cross'.

Clarke wanted the celebration to be completed early so he could leave for a family function. But according to *The Daily Telegraph*, it became nasty when Katich grabbed the then vice-captain Clarke by the throat and the two had to be pulled apart by teammates.

'Yes, we had a disagreement after the Sydney Test,' Clarke told the newspaper:

This kind of thing occasionally happens in cricket teams. We didn't see eye to eye on that night, but we have been teammates at New South Wales and Australia a long time. We've spoken since, including catching up the other night at the Allan Border Medal [2009]. There's no issue between us.

Katich agreed with Clarke saying, 'Michael and I are focused on some tough Test cricket that's coming up for Australia against South Africa in a couple of weeks.'

End of the story? Far from it! On 28 October 2011, Katich suggested that his dressing-room stoush with Clarke two years previously had contributed to his being dropped from the Australian side. After scoring a Sheffield Shield century in 2011, Katich was asked, according to *Cricinfo*, whether the appointment of a new chairman of selectors, John Inverarity, would help his cause in winning a recall, 'It's pleasing to hear but I think you don't have to be Einstein to figure out that it's not just the selectors that had a part in sending me on my way,' Katich said. 'I mean to be brutally honest; obviously what happened in the dressing room here a few years ago didn't help my cause. And obviously the captain and coach are selectors.'

When asked if he could expect to play for Australia again while Clarke remained captain, Katich said: 'I wouldn't have thought so. That's probably why I'm in this position in the first place.'

At a disciplinary hearing, Katich escaped suspension from Cricket Australia (CA) for his remarks against Clarke after pleading guilty at a CA Code of Behaviour hearing, chaired by retired county court judge Gordon Lewis in Melbourne and was handed an official reprimand.

Captaining Australia, Clarke had a marvellous Test series against India in 2011–12 winning 4–0 and scoring 626 runs at 125.20, highlighted with a superb unbeaten 329 in Sydney. A disillusioned Katich retired from first-class cricket in Australia in June 2012.

STANFORD JAILED FOR 110 YEARS

We realise that human life expectancy is rising every year but a jail sentence of 110 years for former Texan billionaire Allen Stanford, 62, appears strange. This means he will be released when he touches 172. Ridiculous? Then listen to this. The prosecutors had asked for a jail term of 230 years, when he would be a free man at 292! Call me a legal ignoramus but doesn't it get curious and curiouser?

Not that he does not deserve a long jail sentence. Why not imprison him *for life* for one of the biggest frauds in history? But at times, logic and legalities are poles apart.

Stanford, the disgraced Texan financier, came on the cricket scene in the last decade promising riches to English and West Indian cricket. He was hailed as the saviour of Caribbean cricket when he bankrolled an international cricket tournament in Antigua that promised to improve the finances in England and the West Indies cricket, and become a rival to the money-spinning Indian Premier League.

The deal had been publicised in ostentatious style as Stanford was allowed to land his private helicopter on the outfield at Lord's, after which he presented a Perspex box filled with A$20 million (about £13 million) in prize money in front of the smiling England and Wales Cricket Board (ECB) officials. Stanford signed a 5-year contract with the ECB worth A$100 million (about £64 million).

But his financial empire collapsed under an investigation by the United States regulators. Since his arrest in 2009, he spent three years in jail after he was denied bail. He was convicted on 13 of 14 charges against him as he was found guilty of defrauding investors of more than 7 billion dollars.

Stanford, whose trial was delayed on health grounds after he was beaten up by prison inmates, has always denied his guilt and told the District Judge David Hittner at his court hearing: 'I did not defraud anybody.'

He stuck to his claim that he did not run a Ponzi scheme—a fraudulent investment operation that pays returns to its investors from their own money or the money paid by subsequent investors, rather than from profit earned by the individual or organisation, and that his financial affairs only collapsed once investigations into his affairs became known.

He told the judge, 'I'm not here to ask for sympathy or forgiveness or to throw myself at your mercy. I did not run a Ponzi scheme. I didn't defraud anybody.'

It looked a dawn of a new prosperous era in 2008 when England and West Indies contested a Twenty20 match in Antigua for a winner-takes-all prize of £20 million. 'Stanford socialised in a touchy-feely fashion with England players' wives, waved to the crowds, entered the dressing rooms at will and finished the night with what was virtually an impromptu cabaret', according to a report in *Cricinfo*. But his multimillion cricketing 'empire' collapsed in a heap with the financier in jail.

Perhaps this is an ideal way to conclude a book on con-flicts and con-troversies, with a prolonged imprisonment of a 'con-man'. The take home message is: the more things change, the more they remain the same. Going down memory lane, was the game any better for the controversies, briberies, gambling, mud-slinging in the 19th century as it is now? Greed for excessive money has led players astray, from Ted Pooley in 1876 to quite a few of today's *crorepati* (multimillionaire) cricketers.

A mystic Indian poet Kabir (born 1440) wrote these famous lines, which when roughly translated in English mean: 'A man may have wealth of cattle and elephants, women, diamonds and gold mines. But if he does not have contentment, all these riches are like dust.'

BIBLIOGRAPHY

BOOKS

Bala, R 1970, *Kiwis and Kangaroos – India* 1969, The Statesman, India.

Benaud, R 1998, *Anything but... An Autobiography,* Coronet Books, Hodder & Stoughton, UK.

Bose, M 1990, *A History of Indian Cricket*, André Deutsch Ltd., UK.

Botham, I 1982, *The Incredible Tests*, 1981, Pelham Books, UK.

Bradman, D 1950, *Farewell to Cricket*, Hodder & Stoughton, UK.

Browning, M 1996, Richie Benaud. *Cricketer, Captain, Guru*, Kangaroo Press, Australia.

Cashman, R 1980, *Patrons, Players and the Crowd – The Phenomenon of Indian Cricket*, Orient Longman's Ltd., India.

Cashman, R, Maxwell, J, Stoddart, B, Weaver, A, Webster, R, Franks, W 1996, The Oxford Companion to Australian Cricket, Oxford University Press, Australia.

Chappell, G 2011, Fierce Focus, Hardie Grant Books, UK.

Chappell, I, Robertson, A, Rigby, P 1981, *Chappelli laughs again, Cricket's funniest stories*, Lansdowne Press, Australia.

Coward, M 2004, *Bookies, Rebels & Renaissance – Cricket in the 80s*, ABC Books, Australia.

Crowley, B 1984, *Cricket Exiles – The Saga of South African Cricket*, Angus & Robertson Publishers, UK.

D'Oliveira, B & Murphy, P 1969, *The D'Oliveira Affair*, Harper Collins, UK.

de Moore, G 2008, Tom Wills, *His Spectacular Rise and Tragic Fall*, Allen & Unwin, Australia.

Derriman, P 2012, *100 TESTS: A Century of Test Match Cricket at the Sydney Cricket Ground*, Playwright Publishing, Australia. To be released.

Derriman, P 1984, *Bodyline – The Day England Declared War on Australia*, Fontana Books, Australia.

Dunne, S & Edwards, B 2003, *Alone in the Middle: An Umpire's Story*, Penguin, UK.

Eason, A 2008, *The A–Z of Bradman*, Scribe Publications, Australia.

Fingleton, J 1981, *Batting from Memory*, HarperCollins, Australia.

Fingleton, J 1972, *Fingleton on Cricket*, Collins, UK.

Frindall, B (ed.) 1979, *The Wisden Book of Test Cricket*, 1876–77 to 1977–78, Macdonald and Jane's Publishers Ltd., UK.

Frindall, B (ed.) 1995, *The Wisden Book of Test Cricket*, Vol. II, 1977–1994, Headline Book Publishing, UK.

Frith, D 2002, *Bodyline Autopsy*, Australian Broadcasting Corporation, Australia.

Gavaskar, S 1983, *Idols*, Rupa Paperback, India.

Gavaskar, S 1984, *Runs and Ruins*, Rupa Paperback, India.

Gavaskar, S 1976, *Sunny Days*, Rupa & Co., India.

Gilchrist, A 2008, *True Colours – My Life*, Pan Macmillan, Australia.

Green, B (comp.) 1986, *The Wisden Book of Cricketers' Lives*, Queen Anne Press, UK.

Growden, G 2008, *Jack Fingleton – The Man who Stood Up to Bradman*, Allen & Unwin, Australia.

Haigh, G 1993, *The Cricket War: The Inside Story of Kerry Packer's World Series*, Melbourne Text Publishing, Australia.

Hair, D 1998, *Decision Maker – An Umpire's Story*, Random House, Australia.

Hair, D 2011, *In the Best Interests of the Game*, Harper Collins, Australia.

Harold, J 2008, *The Art of Sledging*, Allen & Unwin, Australia.

Harte, C & Hadfield, W 1985, *Cricket Rebels*, QB Book, Australia.

Jenkins, D 2009, *Near Death on the Sub-continent – The Gavin Stevens Story*, The Cricket Publishing Company, Australia.

Knight, J 2002, *Mark Waugh – the Biography*, HarperSports, Australia.

Knox, M 2009, *The Greatest – the players, the moments, the matches – 1993–2008*, Hardie Grant Books, UK.

Lillee, D 1982, *Lillee – My Life in Cricket*, Methuen, Australia.

Lillee, D 1984, *Over and Out*, Methuen, Australia.

Lloyd, C 1980, *Living for Cricket*, Stanley Paul & Co. Ltd., UK.

Majumdar, B 2004, *Once upon a Furore*, Yoda Press, India.

Martin–Jenkins, C 1996, *World Cricketers – A Biographical Dictionary*, Oxford University Press, UK.

McFarline, P 1977, *A Game Divided*, Hutchinson Group, Australia.

Meckiff, I & McDonald I, 1961, *Thrown Out*, Stanley Paul, UK.

Meher–Homji, K, 2008, *Cricket's Great All-rounders*, New Holland Publishers, Aus., NZ, Eng.,SAf.

Meher–Homji, K 2001, *Dramatic Debuts and Swan Songs*, ABC Books, Australia.

Meher–Homji, K 2003, *Heroes of 100 Tests*, Rosenberg Publishing, Australia.

Meher–Homji, K 1993, *Out for a Duck*, Kangaroo Press, Australia.

Menon, S 2011, *Bishan – Portrait of a Cricketer*, Penguin, India.

Mukherjee, S 1968, *The Romance of Indian Cricket*, Hind Pocket Books, India.

Mulvaney, R & Harcourt, R 1988, *Cricket Walkabout: The Australian Aborigines in England*, McMillan, Australia.

Odendaal, André (ed.) 1997, *Cricket in Isolation – The Politics of Race and Cricket in South Africa*, André Odendaal, SAf.

Odendaal, André (ed.) 1976, *God's Forgotten Cricketers*, South African Cricketer, SAf.

Piesse, K 2001, *Cricket's Greatest Scandals*, Penguin Books Aus. Ltd., Australia.

Pollard, J 1982, *Australian Cricket – The Game and the Players*, Hodder & Stougton, Australia.

Pollard, J 1992, *The Complete Illustrated History of Australian Cricket*, Pelham Books, Australia.

Richards, B 1978, *The Barry Richards Story*, Faber & Faber Ltd., UK.

Robinson, R 1979, *The Wildest Tests*, Castle Australia, Ltd., Australia.

Rowan, L 1972, *The Umpire's Story*, Jack Pollard Pty. Ltd., Australia.

Simpson, B 1966, *Captain's Story*, Hutchinson Group, Australia.

Simpson, B 1977, *Captain's Story*, Marlin edition, Australia.

Tatz, C 1995, *Obstacle Race: Aborigines in Sport*, University of NSW Press, Australia.

Warne, S & Hobson, R (ed.) 2001, *Shane Warne – My Autobiography*, Hodder & Stoughton, UK.

Waugh S 2005, *Out of My Comfort Zone – the Autobiography*, Penguin Group, Australia.

Webster, R (comp.) 1997, *First–class Cricket in Australia* – Vol. 2, 1945–46 to 1976–77, Ray Webster, Australia.

Webster, R (comp.) & Miller, A (ed.) 1991, *First–class Cricket in Australia*, Vol. 1, 1850–51 to 1941–42, Ray Webster, Australia.

Wilde, S 1998, *Number One: The World's Best Batsmen and Bowlers*, Gollancz, UK.

Wisden Cricketers' Almanack (Many editions—latest by John Wisden & Co. Ltd., UK, 2012).

WEBSITES

Cricinfo (www.cricinfo.com)
The Roar (www.theroar.com.au)

MAGAZINES / DAILIES

The Daily Telegraph (Aus.)
Daily Telegraph (UK)
Hindustan Times (Ind.)
Inside Cricket (Aus.)
Inside Sport (Aus.)
Mid–Day (Ind.)
The Australian (Aus.)
The Gleaner (Jamaica, WI)
The New Age (SAf.)
The Sun–Herald (Aus.)
The Sydney Morning Herald (Aus.)
The Wisden Cricketer (UK)
Wisden Cricket Monthly (UK)

ACKNOWLEDGEMENTS

I am grateful to Greg Chappell for writing an excellent Foreword.

I also would like to thank:
Fiona Schultz, Alan Whiticker, Michele Perry, Diane Ward, Evin Priest, Lliane Clarke and others at New Holland Publishers for their help; Bruce Edgar, Warwick Franks, Ian Chappell, Ashley Mallett, Brian Taber, Glenn Turner, Bishan Bedi, Phil Derriman, Mike Coward, Gulu Ezekiel, David Jenkins, Jason Ford and Bipin Dani for sharing their experiences and making valuable comments; Colin Clowes and Bob Brenner from NSW Cricket Association Library for helping me refer to rare publications for my research; Ronald Cardwell, the founder of the Australian Cricket Society, NSW, and Phil Derriman for providing rare photographs.

First published 2012 by
New Holland Publishers Pty Ltd
London • Sydney • Cape Town • Auckland

Garfield House 86–88 Edgware Road London W2 2EA United Kingdom
1/66 Gibbes Street Chatswood NSW 2067 Australia
218 Lake Road Northcote Auckland New Zealand
Wembley Square First Floor Solan Road Gardens Cape Town 8001 South Africa

www.newhollandpublishers.com

A record of this book is held at the British Library and National Library of Australia

ISBN 9781742573304

Publisher: Alan Whiticker
Publishing director: Lliane Clarke
Designer: Yamin Spendlove, Kimberley Pearce
Cover design: Tracy Loughlin
Editor: Michele Perry
Editorial Assistant: Evin Priest
Production director: Olga Dementiev
Printed and bound by CPI Group (UK) Ltd, Croydon, CR0 4YY

10 9 8 7 6 5 4 3 2 1

Keep up with New Holland Publishers on Facebook http://www.facebook.com/NewHollandPublishers

£ 14.99